ANTONÍN DVOŘÁK

OTAKAR ŠOUREK

THE CHAMBER MUSIC

OF

ANTONÍN DVOŘÁK

OTAKAR ŠOUREK

ENGLISH VERSION
BY
ROBERTA FINLAYSON SAMSOUR

ARTIA

Designed and produced by
A R T I A
Printed in Czechoslovakia

CONTENTS

LIST OF ILLUSTRATIONS:

DVOŘÁK'S CHAMBER MUSIC

In the unusually rich and widely varied musical creation of Antonín Dvořák (8. IX. 1841—1. V. 1904), chamber music holds an
important place in respect of both the number and the artistic value
of the chamber works which came from his pen.

And justly so. If we but take a survey of these intimate creations
of the great Czech composer and recall the rare enjoyment which
their pure and elevating beauty awakens in the listener, we cannot
fail to feel the deepest and sincerest admiration for the truth of such
an art. For Dvořák, in spite of all his emotional complexity and
nobility of character, was remarkably simple, a man of the people,
with all the best traits of the class from which he sprang. Yet he was
able to direct his overflowing musicality into one of the fields of
absolute music making the highest and most complex demands on
the author and one which he cultivated from his earliest beginnings
throughout a period of no less than thirty-five years. And our admiration is mingled with respect when we realize, as in the case of
Dvořák's enthusiastic love for the symphonic form, what creative
daring and independence was shown by an artist who, in spite of
the powerful attraction which the great musical Neo-Romanticists,
Wagner and Liszt, had for him, did not allow them to influence him
except in minor ways, nor was afraid by his persistent adherence to
the cyclic and classical forms of pure, non-programme music to dis-
regard the fundamental slogans of Neo-Romanticism which at that
time held sway, even at the risk of his art being labelled by his con-
temporaries as unprogressive. In his creative work Dvořák went his
own independent way and seldom looked aside to consider what
this or that one thought of it. In satisfying his strong predilection
for chamber music, he had at his disposal the essential artistic
pre-requisites. His reflective, introspective and reserved nature
found, especially in chamber music, the artistic medium most suited
to his own intimate spiritual experiences, whether of a happier or

more melancholy kind, to which he needed to give expression independent of any extra-musical scheme, but also without the em-
ployment of any ostentatious musical means. And secondly, as an
artist of true genius in the fertility, strength and freshness of his in-
born musicality and in the power to work up his ideas with the help
of a rich and wide range of technical resources, employed with
spontaneous and free-flowing originality, he was able, though not
without an initial struggle, to find the proper response to the stylistic demands of chamber music, to appreciate the delicacy of its
compositional structure, and to respect it alike in the character of
the content and treatment as also in the compass of the tone-values.

As regards the thematic material, Dvořák could, moreover, draw
upon the same source as for his whole creative production: an inexhaustible wealth of fresh, delightfully charming or strikingly original melodic, rhythmic and harmonic ideas. All these together
create here, too, a splendid basis for the composer's artistic expression, especially when originality and beauty of thought is yoked with
a refinement and elevation of expression which is, for chamber
music, an indispensible attribute. A much weightier problem for
Dvořák's creative spirit was the organic working up and formal
mastery of this material, and, indeed, he had to wage a truly hard
and stubborn struggle for the mastery of the sonata form, of which
several of his earliest chamber works bear clear traces. This struggle,
however, proved very beneficial and productive, and ended in
victory; that is, it cleared the path of advance to full creative maturity, so that Dvořák showed himself to be, in chamber music, an
equally outstanding master in musical composition as he had earlier
shown himself to be in the magic beauty of his instrumentation.
Here, too, his work is devoid of any striving after effect for its own
sake, and yet, despite all its naturalness, is astonishingly pure, rich
and colourful.

While there is no doubt that, in the forming of Dvořák's musical
individuality of expression after the initial phases of dependence on

Classical, Romantic and Neo-Romantic models had been overcome, Smetana's creative example exercised a very considerable
influence. It is equally certain that, however, in the art of clear,
logical treatment of thematic material, and of building up a well-
proportioned and plastic musical structure, his teacher was first
Beethoven, up to the period of the "Rasumovsky" Quartets (op. 59)
and then Johannes Brahms, who not only gave the young Czech
composer valuable advice but was also his sincere friend. These
influences and this development are as apparent in Dvořák's chamber music as they are in his symphonic compositions, and all the
more so as in neither did he seek to create new forms but kept to the
well-established classical forms. He did not, however, adhere to them
by any means slavishly, following in general only the main features
of the scheme while allowing himself, as always, freedom to make any
divergences or changes as were dictated by the specific musical
content of the work. In chamber music, too, Dvořák's compositional
inventiveness is documented most clearly in the great structural
variety of the opening and closing movements, whether written in
sonata or rondo form, although the question of structure was, at
first, a problem with which his lively and unusually fertile imagination had experienced not a few hard tussles. An outstanding feature of Dvořák's chamber music are the middle movements—the
slow movement and the scherzo, which are as a rule distinguished
by their high artistic values. Indeed, of the majority of the former it
may be affirmed that they are among the loveliest slow movements
in the whole literature of chamber music. They are a measure of
Dvořák's imaginative sense of beauty and the broad melodiousness
of his musical inspiration as well as of the emotional wealth, the
passionate longings, the noble religious fervency and the deep con-
templativeness of his spiritual life.

The Scherzo movements, drawing effectively on the artist's ele-
mental sense of rhythm, are in his chamber music, too, fresh, not
seldom overflowing with high spirits, and separated by idyllic

intermezzos in which a Czech *furiant, polka* or *sousedská* often provide the substitute for the traditional classical dance. They are all manifestations of strong originality and of a full-blooded and positive love of life. In addition, the Slavonic core of Dvořák's make-up finds expression in his chamber music in art stylisations of the *Dumka*, which is here raised to an art form of unusual originality and beauty.

Antonín Dvořák's collection of chamber-music works (excluding his two Serenades) comprises no less than 31 compositions. Among them the largest single group are the string quartets, of which there are 14 or little under half of the total. There are 10 compositions for ensembles including the piano (2 Quintets, 2 Quartets, 4 Trios, a Sonata and a Sonatina), the remaining works being for different string ensembles (Sextet, 3 Quintets, 2 Tercets), while 1 composition is written for two violins, violoncello and harmonium ("Bagatelles").

A chronological survey of Dvořák's numerous chamber works gives a very instructive picture of the artist's creative development from its very beginnings to almost the last years of his life. It is somewhat surprising that Dvořák's first two compositions belong to this field and that quite a number date from the time when the composer was still unknown or practically so, that is, previous to 1873. Surprising, because we must realize that in the sixties and seventies of the last century, when these compositions were being written, performances of chamber music in Prague were quite irregular and comparatively rare, being restricted to occasional concerts by ensembles which, as a rule, were only very short-lived. The repertoire of these ensembles was also narrow in its range and confined to the greatest names in Classical and Romantic Music (Haydn, Mozart, Beethoven, Schubert, Schumann, Spohr etc.). Dvořák, as an unknown viola player in the Interim Theatre orchestra, could entertain little hope of engaging their attention when he failed to do so even later as a successful composer of symphonies and cantatas.

It is sufficient to cite the fact that the first public performance of his first string quartet took place towards the end of 1878 when he was already at work on his tenth (!) quartet and when among them were works of a quality such as won fame for their author all over the world as, for example, the quartets in E major, D minor and E flat major.

We have, therefore, more than sufficient grounds for the belief that Dvořák's fondness for chamber music was spontaneous, and originated alone in the urgent need of his creative being to express itself in this intimate and for him particularly congenial form of musical composition. This inner necessity explains why his first serious composition after finishing his studies at the Prague Organ School was a String Quintet with two violas in A minor, op. 1 (1861), and why his next composition was his first String Quartet in A major op. 2 (1862). Both compositions prove how much Dvořák learned from the works of the Classical and the Romantic masters which were the only chamber compositions he had the opportunity to hear performed, and especially those of Mozart, Beethoven and Schubert. And though these first compositions are inventively still in great measure derivative and show as yet considerable uncertainty in the command of the sonata form, there is already apparent in them the romantic vigour and freshness of youth and, above all, the promise of high gifts in the musical ideas and treatment.

Three of Dvořák's string quartets date from the end of the sixties and beginning of the seventies, the first in D major, the second in E minor and the third in B flat major, all interesting as arising in close, chronological proximity to his first opera, "Alfred", and at a time when Dvořák was most strongly under the spell of Richard Wagner and Franz Liszt, so that they bear in a number of respects clear traces of the influence of the great Neo-Romanticists. These are reflected partly in the character of the inventive material, but especially in the diffuseness and lack of proportion and balance in the musical structure, the struggle for which seems here to be in its

most critical phase. The E minor Quartet and also the expressively
nearly related Sonata for Violoncello and Piano in F minor, which
was written immediately afterwards (of which only the 'cello part is
extant), are of interest as being not only Dvořák's first, but also the
first Czech works in the sphere of absolute music in which the individual movements of the cyclic form constitute, in accordance
with Liszt's example, an organic whole. (As no further reference
will be made to these works, the opportunity is taken here to note
that from the slow middle movement of the E minor Quartet there
arose the later well-known Notturno for string orchestra op. 40.)

The struggle for mastery of form, especially of sonata form, which
had its beginnings in the works mentioned above, continued
throughout several subsequent chamber compositions from the
years 1872 and 1873, but with perceptible progress from one work
to the next along with equally perceptible advances towards individuality of musical expression. This group of compositions includes the first Piano Quintet in A major op. 5, (not to be confused
with the famous quintet in the same key, op. 81!) and then two new
string quartets, the first in F minor and the second in A minor (op.
12). In these works, too, there are still signs of considerable ferment
in respect of form and structure, but there is nevertheless a clear
striving after structural and expressive cohesiveness and an indisput-
able advance in the inventiveness and originality of the musical
content. Progress in this direction can best be gauged by the post-
humous F minor Quartet, the most original of the three works,
while the well-known Romance for violin accompanied by a small
orchestra (or piano) op. 11, written somewhat later, was based on its
slow movement. The second of the quartets,—the one in A minor,—
is interesting as being the last and the most daring and also the least
successful attempt at the formal unification of the individual parts
of a cyclic composition, and as providing the first example of the
composer's use of the variation form in chamber music. Unfortun-
ately the composition has not survived complete.

The turning-point in Dvořák's struggle for mastery of form is marked by a humble return to strictly traditional forms, now completely under control, as is convincingly demonstrated by the next String Quartet, in A minor op. 16. (1874), composed shortly after the A minor Quartet op. 12. Proof that it was not reached without a struggle is apparent from the fact that, in the new Quartet, balance of form and structural design were achieved at the price of putting a strong curb on his imaginative invention. Dvořák, however, was very soon able to prove that such restraint was only a passing phase and the last hurdle on the road to complete artistic independence of expression. A happy proof that this was so is the String Quintet with double-bass in G major, dating from the beginning of 1875. It contained the first of Dvořák's lovely Adagios, and followed close on the preceding quartet as op. 18 (Simrock published it against the author's will under the deceptively high opus number 77), to be followed by several chamber works written in relatively quick succession in the same year, 1875, and the following year. They include two Piano Trios, one in B flat major, op. 21, and the other in G minor, op. 26, both full of youthful vitality, the first with greater fighting élan, the second more yearningly introspective, then the very intimate Piano Quartet in D major, op. 23, in three movements, with a lovely middle movement in the form of variations, and, finally, the eighth String Quartet, this time in the key of E major, the original opus number 27 being later changed by Simrock to op. 80. In all these compositions, beginning with the Quintet with double-bass, there sounds, with growing clarity and emphasis, the characteristic tone of Dvořák's artistically maturing personality with its increasingly definite national colouring. The E major Quartet, which opens the series of Dvořák's greatest and most famous quartets, is also notable for its miniature slow movement, the Slav melancholy of whose mood is a precursor of the later so typical "Dumky", with their alternating moods of pensive contemplation and boisterous high spirits.

An important bent was given at this time to Dvořák's creative production by contact with Brahms's musical works and later with Brahms himself. It was the Viennese Master, it will be remembered, who having become acquainted with Dvořák's works in the first half of the seventies, as a member of the Adjudicating Board for State Grants set up by the former Austro-Hungarian Goverment, and being sincerely impressed by his contributions, in 1877 successfully recommended the as yet unknown Czech composer to his Berlin publisher, Simrock, and remained his whole life Dvořák's admirer and personal friend. This intimacy between the two artists was reflected in the influence exercised by each on the other's creative work. As regards Dvořák, it must be said that an attentive study of Brahms's works helped him to develop the art of thematic treatment, of greater rhythmic individualisation and differentiation of the themes themselves and of the better internal design of the individual movements in the relations of their constituent parts, that is, especially in those features which contribute to the architectonic expressiveness and plasticity of the musical content and to aesthetic refinement of form. The beginnings of Dvořák's contact with Brahms and his work are reflected very clearly in the sphere of chamber music in his ninth String Quartet in D minor, op. 34, which arose shortly before Brahms's recommendation of Dvořák to Simrock (end of 1877), and is also dedicated to Brahms (see quotation from the dedicatory letter on page 78). It is a work of rare chamber music intimacy and refinement, revealing true mastery in all aspects of the compositional art and documenting the composer's national individuality not only in the character of certain musical ideas but also in the idealisation of the Czech polka in the parallel parts of the Scherzo movement and of the "Sousedská" in the middle section.

At the beginning of 1878, Simrock published the Moravian Duets and the first series of "Slavonic Dances", whose quite exceptional success made the modest Czech composer world famous almost over night. In addition to their freshness, spontaneity and fertility of invention, it was above all the unmistakably national tone of these compositions which won them in Germany and other countries such a decided success. It was, therefore, natural that Dvořák should lay special emphasis on the national colouring of his musical expression in his new chamber compositions, which very soon awakened the lively interest of the most celebrated ensembles of the day. Certain of their movements are art stylisations of characteristic Czech song and dance types (the *furiant, polka, sousedská, skočná*) and the Slav "dumka", besides which his musical invention was at this time in especially close contact with the sources of Czech and Moravian folk music. This is reflected not in the direct use of their melodies, but in the way he imparts to his own musical thoughts their pure and individual fragrance, their depth and emotional naiveté and also a number of their melodic and harmonic features (as, for instance, the closing in the relative minor key of a melodic period in the major key, or the other way about, or the characteristic shift of key to a lower second etc.).

In this so called "Slavonic" period, the first little work we meet with is as charming as the combination of instruments for which it is written is unusual. It is the "Bagatelles" for two violins, violoncello and harmonium, op. 47, composed in the Spring of 1878. Dvořák's creative maturity is all the more apparent in proportion to the degree of modesty and intimacy which characterises the work. The most outstanding chamber works of this period, however, are undoubtedly the String Sextet in A major, op. 48, from the spring of 1878 and the String Quartet in E flat major op. 51 (the tenth in the order of composition), from the beginning of 1878, the former making its way into the world in the interpretation of the celebrated Joseph Joachim Quartet, and the latter thanks to the equally famous Florentine Quartet led by Jean Becker, at whose request the quartet was composed and to whom it is dedicated. Both compositions have the pungent fragrance of Czech meadows in flower: not a thought but is a colourful national ornament, not a mood but is the expression of simple deep human emotions carried on a stream of ardent melody and fiery rhythms, at a time when Dvořák's soul was full to overflowing with the inner happiness that, after such long neglect and privation, his first great successes in the world had brought him. The Sextet is in structure and tone-texture more robust, the Quartet more intimate and delicate. In both compositions the second movement is a "dumka", figuring in the Sextet as the slow movement and in the Quartet as the Scherzo, while in the Sextet the Scherzo is designated a furiant and in the Quartet the last movement a Czech "skočná".

A composition perhaps relatively less characteristic and musically significant is the Sonata in F major for violin and piano, in three movements, op. 57, dating from 1880—a work of idyllic refinement and with Brahmsian colouring in the first two movements. It stands at the threshold of the next phase of Dvořák's creation in which thoughts generated by the spirit of Czech folk music acquire, in passing through the prism of the artist's creative personality, a more subtly distilled and personally crystallized form, the term "national" being transformed into something specifically "Dvořák". Dvořák's artistic work here enters the phase of summer maturity, significant testimony in the sphere of chamber music being the String Quartet in C major op. 61, composed at the end of 1881 and dedicated to the Viennese quartet leader Joseph Hellmesberger a composition which, despite the poetic quality of its musical thoughts and its remarkable expressive force, holds a somewhat special place in this culminating phrase of Dvořák's chamber music because of the spiritualised and unearthly quality both of the content and mood in which it approaches most strikingly to the classicism of Beethoven. And even the delightful scherzo, a movement usually so characteristically Dvořák, is purely classic in line, while its lovely trio displays itself with a more Schubertian sweetness and charm. This work is immediately followed by the Piano Trio in F minor, op. 65, from 1883, a work which is almost unique in Dvořák's chamber music in the darkly passionate character of its musical content and artistically reflecting that period in the life and creation of the composer when he was inwardly disturbed and irritated by the conflict between his desire to make a name for himself abroad, also in the field of operatic composition, and yet remain true to his national mission as an artist. The power of the stubborn doubts and tormenting uncertainty which warred in Dvořák's soul at this time is truthfully reflected in the wide scale of moods and emotional strength and beauty of the Trio in F minor, which rank it among the most significant of the master's chamber works.

Out of this mood arose the powerful D minor Symphony, op. 70, which was otherwise alien to Dvořák's optimistic disposition. Proof that it was no more than an intermezzo which ended in a victorious rejection of all foreign enticements is forthcoming in a number of delightful chamber music works. Among these smaller and relatively simple works, composed with an almost impromptu lightness of touch and charm of tone colouring, are two "Tercets" for two violins and viola (1887), of which the first in C major (op. 74) is well-known, while the second was long supplanted by the composer's arrangement of it for violin and piano under the title "Romantic Pieces", (op. 75). And following them, as works of high musical value and artistic significance, are the Piano Quintet in A major, op. 81, also written in 1887, and the Piano Quartet in E flat major, op. 87, from the year 1889, the former more varied and rambling, the second more closely-knit and somehow manly, both, however, displaying the full range of the composer's genius in the beauty and expressiveness of musical ideas and in the imaginative resource apparent in the compositional design and instrumentation. The inner connection with the earlier "Slavonic" period of Dvořák's creative production is maintained in the Quintet by the Dumka which represents the slow movement and by the Furiant as the Scherzo. The above-mentioned Dumka, as also the slow movement in the Piano Quartet, are among the choicest of Dvořák's musical lyrics. Dvořák's fondness for the dumka form was also reflected very strongly in the organically unified cycle of six of these very characteristic movements in the form of a Piano Trio, to which he also gave the designation "Dumky", op. 90 (1890), and which is a work of undoubted charm and originality.

The next three chamber works to come from Dvořák's pen form a special group as being composed during Dvořák's sojourn in America and also because they not only reflect the vivid impressions of his new surroundings and contacts, but also have in common many of those characteristic features which gave a specific colouring to Dvořák's compositions under the influence of American folk songs, original or adopted, and especially those of the Negro population, a more detailed reference to which will be made in the analysis of the works in question. The group comprises the String Quartet in F major, op. 96, the String Quintet with two violas E flat major, op. 97, and the Sonatina in G major for Violin and Piano, op. 100. All three compositions arose in 1893—the Quartet and Quintet in the summer vacation which Dvořák spent with his family in the farming settlement of Spillville, Iowa, and the Sonatina in December in New York, shortly before the historic success of the first performance of the "From the New World" Symphony. The intimate mood of all three works derives from the character of the artist's experiences at the time, while the expressive means are affected as indicated above by the special environment in which they arose, and which undoubtedly introduced into Dvořák's chamber music a new, expressively significant and also attractive note.

The two works which provide a worthy termination to Dvořák's creative production in the field of chamber music and set a crown on the composer's achievement in this branch of composition are a pair of string quartets, the thirteenth and fourteenth, the first of which is in A flat major (op. 105) and the second in G major (op. 106). Dvořák wrote them one after the other at the end of 1895 as the first compositions after his return home from America, and as the musical expression of his immense happiness at breathing once more the air of his native Bohemia and at being able to enjoy the beauties of the Czech countryside. These are the emotions that inspired his two last chamber works in which all the manly vigour of his creative powers and the ardour of the inner impulse which prompted them combine to create works unusually rich in content and of rare beauty of thought and form. Thus he showed that he was able to complete the imposing and complex structure of his chamber-music composition with two works designed and chiselled with consummate craftsmanship.

That was less than nine years before Dvořák's death. In these last years Dvořák dedicated himself to the creation of symphonic poems and operas, and it was in vain that his publisher begged him to write more chamber works. Dvořák knew that in this field he had said all that his inner urge and obligations as an artist had required of him, and in a way that would ensure him an honourable and lasting name in the world history of chamber music. For Czech music Dvořák's chamber works had this additional significance that they form the massive and truly basic foundations of the art, in as far as they are manifestations of expressive and stylistic features of national individuality, both in respect of content and form. In this sense they are also, as a whole, its greatest pride, and a rich source on which its further development has amply drawn and still continues to draw.

I

COMPOSITIONS FOR SIX INSTRUMENTS

SEXTET IN A MAJOR

for two violins, two violas and two violoncellos. — Opus 48.

Written in score—the first movement completed between May 14th and 20th, the second by May 24th and the third and fourth movements by May 27th 1878.—First performed in Berlin, on June 29th, 1879, by the enlarged Joseph Joachim Quartet (Joachim, Hegemeister, Wirth, Kottek, Hausmann, Diepert).—Published by Simrock, Berlin in September 1879.—Duration: 31 minutes.

The Sextet in A major was written only a month after the author had completed the first series of Slavonic Dances in the interval between the composition of the first two "Slavonic Rhapsodies". It thus belongs to the very middle of that phase of Dvořák's creation in which the composer, having harvested notable sucesses abroad, laid special stress on his national origins by keeping the inventive substance of his art in close contact with the specific character of Czech folk music and by tuning its prevailing mood to that tone of unaffected warmth of feeling, now happily enthusiastic, now yearningly passionate, such as characterises Czech folk poesy. In the Sextet this basic feature is underlined by the slow movement being given, for the first time in Dvořák's chamber music, the character and designation of a "dumka" and the Scherzo that of a "furiant", and is further stressed by the choice of six instruments, which notably strengthens the diversity of the thought and emotional content of the work as well as the glowing colourfulness of its melodic and harmonic elements.

The first movement *(Allegro moderato,* A major, $^4/_4$) is in sonata form and, in spite of the typically Dvořák breadth of thematic treatment, very clear in design. It is also distinguished by an extra-

ordinary emotional fervency and a sweet melodiousness which is
to be felt immediately in the main theme:

1.   Allegro moderato

In the course of the broad ternary elaboration of this theme,
illuminated as it were by warm sunshine, there are intimations of
the subordinate theme which introduces into the movement greater
dynamic and rhythmical animation:

2.   Quasi allegro con brio

Following close on the dynamic culmination of the subordinate
theme, is the final theme marked by a return to the ardently lyrical
tone of the principal subject, which then provides its tender concluding phase.

3.

The exposition dies away with delicate quotations of the subordinate theme (2), which also provides the transition to the development in which lively imitation of this theme is interwoven with
quotations of the principal theme (1). The recapitulation first re-
peats the whole exposition, the only divergence being that the subordinate and closing themes, originally in the unorthodox tonalities
of C sharp minor and C sharp major, are now presented in F sharp
minor and F sharp major. The close of the recapitulation is then
extended to include a vigorous dramatic coda based on the principal
theme alone, a festive augmentation of which brings the movement
to a close.

The second movement is, as noted in the introductory paragraph, entitled "Dumka". Herewith Dvořák took over from piano composition this special form, which derives its name from a Ukrainian folk song in which moods of melancholy retrospection alternate with high-spirited dance sections, and introduced it into his chamber music, returning to it a number of times, and always very happily, till he finally based a whole work on a cycle of six such movements ("Dumky", Piano Trio op. 90, see p. 161). The dumka in the Sextet keeps in the main to three-part rondo form, but with double parallel parts. The first and main part of the latter has the form of a quiet polka, somewhat tinged with melancholy *(Poco Allegretto,* D minor $^2/_4$) with a five-bar theme (4), the second and subordinate part *(Adagio, quasi tempo di marcia,* F sharp minor, $^4/_8$) is a rather sad dance-song with an oriental or, indeed, almost gipsy-like colouring.

The middle part of the movement is a lovely, delicate, dreamy lullaby in the key of F sharp major *(Andante,* $^3/_8$), which develops out of the following tender, charming theme:

The third movement of the Sextet *(Presto,* A major, $^3/_4$) designated by Dvořák as a "furiant", introduces this fiery dance for

the first time into Czech cyclic music. The composer did not use
the designation here with such complete justification as perhaps for
the Scherzo movement of the later D major symphony, its triple
time not alternating here with duple time in the manner so characteristic of this type of Czech dance; but his use of it was quite le-
gitimate if we recall the similar character and rhythmic verve in the
furiant parts of the "Slavonic Dances" with the first of which (in
C major) this composition has also certain affinities of thought. Thus
in the first and extremely fiery part of the Scherzo, the core of which
is this vigorously concise theme:

we come across an allusion to that Dance in the first and following
alternate pairs of bars of the middle auxiliary theme:

And similarly in the Trio, of which the delicacy of expression contrasts strongly with the symmetrical parts, and which develops out
of the theme with its typically Dvořák shift to the relative minor key
at its close:

Yet another figure of the same melody from the first "Slavonic Dance" calls to mind the two-bar phrase which the above-cited theme 9 elaborates in its continuation:*

The fourth movement (*Allegretto grazioso, quasi Andantino*, A major, $^2/_4$) is constructed in the form of variations on the composer's own theme. A pure song-theme of which the predominant mood is one of melancholy meditation, it moves harmonically between B minor, A major and F sharp minor, only brightening up somewhat in the middle with a temporary shift to D and B major:

The variations, of which there are six in all, maintain in general the harmonic character of the theme, but transform its melodic line with imitations of widely varying rhythmic figures and with unfailing imaginative resource in skilfully worked out counterpoints. Thus the first variation combines quavers with triplets, the second moves nimbly in canonic imitation in semi-quavers, the third is a yearning song by the solo violoncello in characteristic rhythm,

* The theme of the above-mentioned "Slavonic Dance", see Ex. 20.

accompanied by sustained notes in the other instruments, the fourth returns to the combination of triplets and quavers, but in a different arrangement, while in the fifth the violins draw a calm, mystically veiled *cantabile* over undulating semi-quaver figurations and the measured steps of pizzicato quavers. The wide range of mood which is a feature shared by all these variations culminates, in the sixth and last, in a broadly designed stretto which concludes the work in a spirit of unconstrained and full-throated rejoicing.

II

COMPOSITIONS FOR FIVE INSTRUMENTS

A. QUINTETS FOR STRING INSTRUMENTS

QUINTET IN A MINOR
for 2 violins, 2 violas and violoncello. — Opus 1.

Written in the summer of 1861 (the score has only one date at the beginning, June 6th, 1861, and at the end only the signature, Antonín Leopold Dvořák).— First performed at a Dvořák Evening held at the Prague Conservatoire on December 15th, 1921. First public performance by the Bohěmian Quartet (Karel Hoffmann, Josef Suk, Jiří Herold, Ladislav Zelenka) and Rudolf Reissig as the second viola at a concert of the Czech Chamber Music Society on February 10th, 1930, in Prague. Published by the Hudební matice Umělecké besedy in Prague, 1943.—Duration: 28 minutes.

The Quintet in A minor is the composition with which Dvořák actually inaugurated his creative work and so also the first link in the imposing series of his chamber works. If we consider of what exceptional importance this creative production was, both in its volume and in its truly incomparable artistic value, we cannot over-look the significance of its beginnings, though such were as yet but a modest presage of what was to come. Nor was it, indeed, anything but natural that the twenty-year-old composer, who had only short-ly before graduated from the organ school and was now employed as a viola player in a private orchestra, should cling in his first work fairly closely to his great classical models—chiefly Mozart and Beethoven and that he should show a typical beginner's uncertainty in the mastery of compositional form. It weighs all the less, in that he revealed, even in this his first serious essay in musical composition, quite unusual creative musical gifts alike in the character of the musical thoughts, expressively melodic and emotionally sincere, and in the stylistically appropriate manner of their structural and instrumental treatment.

The Quintet in A minor consists of three movements, of which the first and last are written in sonata form, the slow middle movement in three-part rondo form (*a b a*). Thus at the very threshold of his creative production, we find one of those cyclic compositions which have no Scherzo, either because its function is absorbed into the quick finale or, as is clearly the case here, because its dancing gaiety of mood is not in keeping with the basic character of the composition.

The first movement has an introduction of fourteen bars (*Adagio*, A minor, ³/₄), in which, after a unison opening and several resolute chords, there rises a calm thought later made use of again in the development:

The actual quick part (*Allegro ma non tropo*, A minor, ⁴/₄) begins straight away with the principal theme, its expression faintly melancholy and reminiscent of Mozart:

The further exposition of this theme concludes with a transitional thought, an interesting pedal point in the inner viola part only underlining the ardent yearning of the opening:

The mood brightens with the entry of the subordinate theme in which violins and viola sing in unison with short interpolations in the 'cello.

This theme, too, is broadly worked out, often with the support of the above-mentioned interpolations by the 'cello (4a), whereupon it turns into the closing theme which—growing out of the inverted final figure of the preceding theme—begins at first timidly, but soon becomes more agitated.

The development, except at the beginning when the calm motif from the slow introduction (1) is repeated several times, works almost exclusively with the elements of the principal theme (2). The recapitulation is normal but, in individual paragraphs, is more discursive and expressively more animated than the exposition. The coda, which winds up the composition, surprises the listener first with its mystic Beethovenesque tranquillity in which the various parts proceed stealthily moving chromatically through a fairly wide tone compass. Thereupon the musical expression becomes strongly agitated but, after a sudden last falling off, the movement ends with a gentle quotation of the opening bars of the principal theme (2).

The second movement *(Lento*, F major, $^3/_4$) is written in symmetrical three part rondo form, all the thoughts being broadly melodic and emotionally ardent. The first viola opens with the principal theme over a rhythmic ostinato accompaniment in the second viola and 'cello, whereupon it is repeated in unison by the violins:

The theme provokes a delicately passionate thought:

which leads to another theme with a broad melodic line:

After an exciting build-up there is a return to the principal theme (6), this time in the key of A major and sung with still greater lyrical intensity. After a number of modulations during which the second theme (8) again appears, there follows the concluding section, the tone-colouring of which is enriched by the repetition of the introductory paragraph, the movement then dying away in a delicate quotation of the subordinate theme.

The third and last movement of the Quintet *(Allegro con brio*, A minor, $^4/_4$) is, as compared with the first movement, decidedly

livelier in mood, though by no means bright or gay. The principal
theme (9) develops out of an energetic figure *(a)* to which in dialogue fashion, figure *(b)* gives a quiet reply.

9.

The subordinate theme is interesting for the way in which it rests
throughout on the third inversion of the chord of the dominant seventh in the relative key of C major with rhythmical intensification
of the pedal point on G in the 'cello:

10.

and only after a third repetition does it settle on its own tonic key
of C major, which proves, however, to be after all only a transitional
key:

A new straightforward transition leads to the final key, its skipping
quaver and semi-quaver rhythm combining and alternating with
triplets:

11.

The broad and interesting processes of the development work up all three basic themes (9, 10, 11). The recapitulation diverges from the original plan only in presenting the subordinate theme in the key of F major (instead of A major) and in giving, in the final section a festive presentation of motif 7 from the preceding slow movement in this variant:

From F major the movement modulates back to the tonic key of A minor only with the return to the closing theme (11), whereupon, after two further culminating passages, the composition ends with an energetic quotation of the principal theme (9a) .

QUINTET IN G MAJOR
for 2 violins, viola, violoncello and double-bass. — Opus 77.

Written at the beginning of 1876 (according to a note in the score "finished in March"), originally as opus 18.—First performed at a concert of the "Umělecká Beseda" on March 18th, 1876, by František Ondříček and members of the musical section of the Beseda.—Published by Simrock, Berlin, 1888 under a new opus number.—Duration: 33 minutes.

The Quintet in G major, generally known as the Quintet with Double-bass, is the first of a group of chamber works which arose in close chronological sequence and in which Dvořák, under the force of Smetana's example, had emancipated himself from the influence of the Neo-Romantists, not only as regards form, in which he had earlier achieved a certain degree of structural concentration and balance, but also as regards expression, in which he was already consciously working his way towards a clearly defined individuality. The Quintet was written very soon after the one-act comic opera, "The Pigheaded Ones", from which the first and third movements have taken over the lively, light and carefree tone but, in beauty of thought and emotional force, are very considerably surpassed by the deeply affecting melodiousness of the slow movement. The Quintet is interesting too, for the combination of a string quartet with double-bass, the use of which allows the composer to write for the higher and lyrically more effective registers of the 'cello, thus giving to the work the special charm of unusual instrumental colouring.

The first movement *(Allegro con fuoco*, G major, ⁴/₄), very fresh and gaily animated in mood, is written in sonata form with two themes. The first of these is short, consisting of only one bar:

Varied and skilful use is made of it throughout the movement, first as a unit and then especially of its second half, from which is developed the motif which opens the repeated part of the expositions:

Its lively pace and characteristic triplets are taken over by the subordinate theme diverging from the traditional scheme by its setting in the key of F major:

The exposition has no closing theme but instead returns to the principal theme (1).

The development discusses both themes, embroidering them with great inventive contrapuntal resource, without, however, any departure from the happy unaffectedness of the basic mood. The recapitulation differs from the exposition in omitting the beginning but expanding the middle section with a new treatment of the main theme 1 and the addition of a specially lively coda drawing for its material upon all the above-quoted themes.

The second movement of the Quintet, the Scherzo *(Allegro vivace*, E minor, ⁶/₈), perhaps the most characteristically Dvořák part of the work, is in three parts *(a b a)*, the outer parts being quite symmetrical. In these the principal theme is interesting, especially for the hopping rhythm of the first two bars alternating with the smooth lullaby movement of the following pair of bars, over which is later drawn the sweetly melting melody of the subordinate theme (4) with the Dvořák modulation to a lower second:*

The Trio section of the Scherzo (C major, ²/₄), very cultivated in its instrumentation and reminiscent, at times, of Beethoven in its line, provides a fairly marked contrast to the parallel section with its quiet, softly pensive mood as well as its interesting harmonic devices. It is fairly broadly built up on this characteristic theme:

* Dvořák took over this modulation from Moravian folk music and was fond of using it. Later it was to give, especially to the Moravian Duets, the spicy fragrance of a musical "dialect".

5.

The third movement *(Poco andante*, C major, $^4/_4$) may be described as one of the most entrancing slow movements in the whole of Dvořák's chamber music creation. It is also ternary in form, but only in the thematic and modulating plan, the middle part being in $^3/_4$ time and set in the key of E major. Otherwise the whole movement is one flowing stream of passionate warmth, depth of feeling and powerfully affecting range of mood. Calm, broad and relatively simple is the theme of the outer sections:

6. Poco andante

the middle theme being of exceptional ardour and beauty of expression especially when it later combines with a counterpoint in the second violin and 'cello or when delivered by the 'cello itself:

7.

As in theme 3 of the preceding Scherzo, it should be noted that the rhythmic ostinato accompaniment of this theme is also derived from the principal theme (6).

The last movement *(Allegro assai*, G major, $^2/_4$) returns to the mood of the first movement but with a considerable intensification of its gay and carefree character. It advances with great dynamic verve, in form of a rondo based on two themes, the exposition of which is followed by a gay kaleidoscope of variants and imitations. The first theme is characterized by an outburst of boisterously irrepressible high spirits, (8) the second is more restrained (9) but the

mischievous demon pops up in the irregular six-bar periodicity as
well as in the stamping rhythms of the last pair of bars:

The basically gay mood of the movement is maintained throughout
its course and holds the attention of the listener with ever new compositional devices, until it rushes with high-spirited verve to its conclusion.

QUINTET IN E FLAT MAJOR
for 2 violins, 2 violas and violoncello. — Opus 97.

Sketch of the first movement begun on June 26th, written in score between
July 1st and 11th; the second in sketch from the 11th and, in score, between
the 12th and 20th July; the third in sketch from the 21st, in score between the
22nd and 27th July, and the fourth in sketch and in score between July, 29th
and August 1st, 1893, all in Spillville in America.—First performed on New
Year's Day 1894, in Boston, at a concert by the Kneisel Quartet (Frank Kneisel, Otto Roth, Louis Svecenski, Alwin Schroeder) with Zach as the second
viola, and in Prague by the Bohemian Quartet (Hoffmann, Suk, Nedbal,
Wihan) with Ferdinand Lachner as the second viola, at a concert of the Czech
Chamber Music Society held on October 10th, 1894.—Published by Simrock,
Berlin, 1894.—Duration: 30 minutes.

The Quintet in E flat major, just as the F major Quartet op. 96
(see p. 96) written immediately before it, expresses Dvořák's impressions during the summer vacation of 1893 in the Czech settlement of Spillville, Iowa. In contrast to the Quartet, which was
the expression of the most intimate spiritual experience, this work

reflects the outward impressions made on the composer by the spirit of the new environment and by some of its very original characters, whose acquiantance the artist made on his frequent excursions into the surrounding forests and prairies.

The prevailing mood of the work is one engendered by a happy and contented state of mind, though in places an undertone of melancholy meditation is perceptible, especially in the slow movement and in the middle section of the Scherzo. As regards the expressive means employed, the Quintet has the features common to most of Dvořák's American compositions and especially prominent in the "From the New World" Symphony and the preceding F major Quartet. They are features which Dvořák became familiar with in Negro spirituals and Indian folksongs or in popularised art songs of the same kind, and, as he expressed it himself, he created a number of his own themes in the same spirit: that is, he employed the pentatonic scale, omitting in the major mode the fourth and seventh degrees and in the minor mode using the diminished seventh (designated in the examples by a cross), while rhythmically he often introduced syncopation, dotted rhythms, etc. Notable in the Quintet, too, is the characteristic drum rhythm which probably arrested Dvořák's attention in the song and dance shows given in Spillville by Indian travelling troupes and which is employed in all the movements except the Larghetto. The strong originality and freshness of the musical ideas, the masterly craftmanship of the compositional art and the inner vitality of the work rank the E flat major Quintet among Dvořák's most popular chamber compositions.

The first movement *(Allegro non tanto*, E flat major, $^3/_4$) is written in normal sonata form, clearly designed and with three main themes in the exposition and recapitulation. The exposition, which is repeated, is preceded by an introduction of twenty-eight bars in which the solo viola anticipates the principal theme 1 with a melancholy augmentation of its opening bars (1 a).

As if sadly disconsolate in its loneliness, the second viola begins a
monologue of sustained melody, the other instruments then joining
in with a diminution of its last pair of bars, the initial mood being
further underlined on the violoncello repeating the whole period
in the soft key E flat minor. The actual exposition then departs very
considerably from the impression of spiritual despondency. It is no
longer evident in the basic shape of the theme (1), with its lively and
flexible melodic line based on the pentatonic scale, and still less is
there any trace of it in its closely following variant 1 b, with its tense
and vigorous Dvořák rhythm.

And if the subordinate theme (2) may still seem to have a faint air
of melancholy about it, the impression is considerably weakened
by the animated drum rhythms which, with almost dance-like
skipping steps, accompany the energetic closing theme (3) delivered
by the viola.

In the development, too, this persistent hopping element gives the impression of continual movement: it skips from one instrument to another, is silent for a while when the principal theme is presented in the bright key of F sharp major, once again breaks in when the viola delivers a yearningly lyrical variant of the same theme, and then almost incessantly disturbs the calm stream of the movement, not being silenced even by the melodic cantilena of the principal theme at the beginning of the recapitulation, which opens straight out into the fiery variant 1 b. It is first shaken off by the coda in which the principal theme sounds forth in a mighty unison of three octaves, but then returns to the melancholy dreamy expression of the introduction, in which mood the movement comes to a quiet close.

The second movement, the Scherzo *(Allegro vivo,* B major, $^2/_2$), spaciously enough designed in three-part rondo form, is strongly affected in its parallel parts by the typical drum rhythm which, however, here assumes quite a different character.

This measured rhythm, with which the solo second viola again opens the movement, has the specific colouring of primitive, exotic music such as tinges the harmonic and rhythmic core of the first Scherzo theme:

4.

Dvořák, however, has ways and means of imparting beauty and nobility to this primitivism. In the second eight-bar strain of this thematic period there arises in the violins a calm, lyrical cantilena woven, as with threads of silvery moonbeams, around the bare contours of the theme:

4 a.

And he knows, too, how to switch from the dominant mood to another, as witness when he quickly follows a double exposition of the first theme with a new theme whose gay thirds and vigorous rhythms are certainly more Czech than primitively exotic:

5.

Whereas the whole first part of the Scherzo, given complete symmetry of design with a new repetition of the first theme, has a predominantly dancing character, the middle part Minore *(Un poco meno mosso*, B minor) is a calm, pensive, slow-moving song. Its theme, one of Dvořák's loveliest, spread over a full thirty-eight bars and derived in its substance from the lyrical motif 4 a, is delivered first of all in the ardent tone of the viola with a pizzicato accompaniment by the other instruments:

6.   Un poco meno mosso

On its repetition, this broadly lyrical theme becomes clearer and brighter in expression due to its shift to the high registers of the violins and also to the rhythmical structure of the accompaniment, in which the second violin animates the situation by a crotchet ostinato derived from theme 4, while both violas join in on the last two beats of each bar with a stereotype figure of four quavers and one crochet.

The third part of the Scherzo is a literal repetition of the first, with the one exception that the exposition of the first theme is expanded by an additional paragraph with a sudden shift to A flat major and that, just before the close, a sudden falling-off in the volume of tone marks the two-fold return, as in reminiscence, of the beginning of the Trio theme (6) in the brighter key of B major.

The third movement *(Larghetto,* A flat minor, $^3/_8$) is in the form of variations on an original theme, which Dvořák had jotted down in his notebook on December 19th, 1892, that is, long before his arrival in America. The depth of mood, in which is faithfully reflected the rich emotional compass and nobility of Dvořák's spirit, along with the rare beauty of its musical contours, make it the crowning glory of the Quintet and one of the most enchanting movements in the whole of the composer's chamber music. In its first section of sixteen bars, which is in the minor mode, it is permeated with an expression of oppressive sadness, both in the opening strain (7a) as well as in the somewhat more passionately animated concluding strain (7b):

In the second section the mood brightens with a modulation to A flat major and also with an expression of ardent yearning underlined by the fact that, in contrast to the American colouring of the first part, there are now audible the unmistakable tones of the composer's native country.

7c.

The variations on this theme, while remaining without exception in the tonic key, exploit to the full the wide compositional possibilities of its melodic and harmonic core. In the first two, the main features are ornamental figurations of the theme in the most varied rhythmical combinations; in the next two the broadly flowing melody of the theme is divided either among different instruments, (third variation) or delivered in the warm tone of the violoncello below a tremolo of the other instruments (the fourth). The fifth and last variation provides the culminating dynamic tension with the rapid runs of its accompanying passages. The movement concludes with a return to the original theme, passionately sonorous in its first strain, and in the second major strain, intimately tender and finally dying away in a delicate cadence-phrase developed from the last pair of bars of the theme.

The fourth movement of the Quintet (Finale, *Allegro giusto*, E flat major, $^2/_2$) is worked out on a fairly broad rondo plan. Its mood is in the main one of rollicking gaiety such as characterizes the three-part principal theme, though the crisp rhythm of its outer periods (8 a) is somewhat modified by the smooth line of the countermelody (8 b):

8a.   Allegro guisto

8b.

The second theme has again an Indian colouring, both in the exotic line of the melody (minor seventh in the minor mode) and in the primitive drum-rhythms of the accompanying pizzicato:

9.

After a partial return to the first theme, there appears another, third theme contrasting with the two preceding themes especially in the tranquillity and warmth of its melody, and if in its pentatonic structure it has also something of that typical "American" quality, the happy exuberance of its development is pure Dvořák:

10.

In strict accordance with the rondo scheme there is a new exposition of the first theme, this time in G flat major, then of the second in E flat minor and, after a new quotation of the first theme in the tonic key of E flat major, the third theme finally makes its appearance, first in B major and then in the tonic basic E flat major. The movement ends with a broadly designed coda in which the gay and vigorous rhythms of the principal theme are worked up to an inimitably Dvořák breath-taking conclusion.

B. QUINTETS FOR STRINGS AND PIANO

QUINTET IN A MAJOR
for 2 violins, viola, violoncello and piano.—Opus 5.

Written in the summer of 1872.—First performed at a musical matinée arranged by Dr Ludevít Procházka on November 22nd, 1872, in the Prague "Konvikt". The players were: Vojtěch Hřímalý, Lederer, Rudolf Krehan, Alois Neruda and Karel ze Sladkovských.—Unpublished.

The first of Dvořák's two piano quintets, both of which are in A major, is unlike the second (op. 81), very little known and dates from the period when the artist was fighting his way out of the stage of greatest ferment, due to his strong partiality for the music of the German-Romanticists, to clarification of expression and creative independence. His overflowing musicality, still not fully under restraint, is responsible for certain structural faults of proportion and balance as well as for an occasional clumsiness in the harmony, but even so it produced a work of singular freshness of invention, cultivated in its subject-matter and convincing in its emotional expressiveness. As regards form, this quintet is interesting as containing only three movements, the mood and partly also the expressive function of the missing scherzo being taken over by the finale.

In the first movement *(Allegro ma non troppo,* A major, $^4/_4$) the prevailing expression is of grave pride mingled with elevated pathos borne on a swift-flowing stream of youthfully passionate élan. This basic mood is announced straight away in the energetic principal theme (1) with which the piano opens the composition and whose proudly courageous attitude is underlined by a modulation from A major to G major, in which key the strings elaborate the theme in rising gradations leading to variant 1 a.

A partial tranquillisation of mood sets in with the episode in F sharp major, rhythmically derived from the close of the principal theme:

The secondary theme with its lightly skipping run-up, imitated in the piano, is not without a touch of humour and introduces a contrasting element of mood:

The closing theme then enters with an equally carefree tone in the first two bars, but is coloured in its further course *(espressivo)* with an expression of passionate emotion:

4.

This theme, too, is repeated without any particular elaboration (with the melody in the violoncello), whereupon a sudden modulation to C major leads to the development. In this section there are reviewed in order the subordinate theme (3), to which rhythmically firm chords in the piano give a somewhat festive character, the principal theme (1) and, finally, the transitional theme (2), which is worked up with elements of other themes and provides the transition to the recapitulation. The latter differs from the exposition mainly in omitting the whole paragraph dealing with the subordinate theme (3) and in the manner in which the closing theme (4), by way of motif 1*a*, builds up into a mighty gradation culminating at the close of the movement in a festively augmented presentation of the principal theme (1).

The second movement *(Andante sostenuto,* F major, ⁴/₄) is very much calmer in mood as compared with the vigour and movement of the opening movement, though it, too, is not without passages of emotional tension. It is opened again by the piano with a broad, grave theme of deep emotional power:

5. **Andante sostenuto**

This theme is then taken over by the violin, with an interesting modulation from the key of F major to that of F sharp minor. The somewhat overcast mood brightens again with the transitional theme presented by the violoncello and the violins:

whereupon a short quotation of the first theme (5) closes the first section of the three-part rondo design.

In the key of G major, which the composer reaches by a sudden modulation through D flat major and the dominant seventh chord from the key of F sharp major, the violoncello sings the subordinate romantic theme over a quaver bass with a fitting rhythmical accompaniment in the piano:

The third part of the movement again works with the principal theme (5), its initial calm being agitated by an expression of tensely passionate emotion but then subsiding and bringing the movement to a delicate conclusion.

The third movement (Finale, *Allegro con brio*, A major, $^6/_8$), despite considerable diffuseness and lack of coherence both in thought-content and mood, is the most original, contrasting with the previous movements in its expression of gay exuberance, and truly puckish in its melodic and rhythmic inventiveness and in its harmonic colouring. In form it combines features of both the sonata and rondo schemes. The beginning is marked by an unexpected stroke—the opening with the harmonically unorthodox dominant seventh chord in B flat major, over which the first theme skips nimbly through a compass of two octaves:

1. Facsimile of the first page from the score of the String Quartet
in A major

2. Facsimile of the first page of the score of the Piano
Quintet in A major

After this theme has run through several diminished chords its elements are worked up in a dynamic gradation at the culmination of which there storms forth a grotesquely coloured chromatic alternation, whereupon a number of resolutely descending steps lead to the playfully nonchalant second theme:

The frolicsome rhythmic and harmonic play of the preceding themes is taken up by the third theme and its variants:

A calmer mood first sets in with the fourth theme, contrasting with the others both in its more lyric character and in its simpler melodic and harmonic structure:

In the course of 140 bars, this theme is developed in relatively simple imitation and modulates successively through the keys of A major, B minor, A major and B major before giving way to the first theme (8), which opens the recapitulation section, its sportive gay mood, except for occasional unexpected reminiscences of the main theme of the first movement (1), rising at the close to a pitch of riotous gaiety.

QUINTET IN A MAJOR
for two violins, viola, violoncello and piano. — Opus 81.

Written in score—the first movement between August 18th and 28th, the other three completed by October 3rd, 1887 (finished "at Vysoká on the Village Feast Day"). Dedicated to University Professor Dr Bohdan Neureuther.— First performed at the eighth popular concert of the "Umělecká beseda" on January 6th, 1888 in Prague. The players were: Karel Ondříček, Jan Pelikán, Petr Mareš, Alois Neruda and Karel Kovařovic.—Published in 1888 by Simrock, Berlin, with a change of the original opus number 77 to number 81.

The second of Dvořák's piano quintets in A major is one of the most delightful and successful chamber works, not only in the composer's works but also in the whole of chamber music composition. The musical content is distinguished by a wealth of lovely melody of glowing colour harmonies and strikingly original rhythms, while its thematic treatment and general design reveal a master of counterpoint and of form. In content the work is the expression of a purely personal lyrical mood such as Dvořák was wont to indulge in after the creative tension demanded by his great oratorios and symphonies. In this work a spirit speaks full of lively sensibilities, full of thoughts freed as it were from the burden of all mundane concerns and wandering in some Elysian Fields of sublime beauty and bliss. A spirit of constantly changing mood, now dreamily pensive or cloudily overcast, now full of joy and radiant happiness.

The first movement *(Allegro ma non tanto*, A major, $^2/_2$) gives in the exposition a picture of all these nuances of mood. The core of the thematic material and treatment consists of only two basic themes; these appear, however, in such a diversity of variants that they determine not only the remarkable changeability of mood but also the typically Dvořák spaciousness of the sonata structure. The principal theme, delivered first by the violoncello to the rocking accompaniment of the piano, is imbued with an expression of melancholy and dreamy pensiveness:

Its first variant, however, brings with it a sudden change of mood, as it energetically spans an octave (instead of the original fourth) above the rapid steps of the accompaniment:

and in its further broadly designed exposition, in which much play is made with the basic rhythm elements, at length breaks into this buoyantly happy variant:

This outburst of happiness, however, subsides as quickly as it arose and a return is made to the principal theme with its original expression of lyrical tranquillity, now, however, emotionally clarified and warmly coloured with a tone of ardent yearning corresponding to the new characteristic development of its second strain:

Yet another change of mood is reflected in the carefree gaiety of the transitional theme, whose running triplets are disturbed by a persistent rhythmic figure out of which the secondary theme is then developed:

2.

This, like the earlier principal theme, is at first tinged with melancholy, but in its broad exposition it becomes increasingly warm in expression in the changing shapes imparted to it by ever new figurations and instrumentation, finally rising at the close of the exposition to a climax of jubilation.

These rapidly alternating moods, reflecting so truthfully Dvořák's emotional mutability, also distinguish the very broadly planned development which shows remarkable resource in the thematic treatment, is withal fresh and spontaneous and deals with all the above-quoted thematic materials in turn. The same quickly alternating moods continue to characterize the recapitulation, which differs from the exposition—apart from the usual shifts of key— only in the emission, at the beginning, of the paragraph containing motifs 1 b and 1 c and in the addition of a short but soaringly jubilant coda.

The second movement of the Quintet is entitled "Dumka" (*Andante con moto*, F sharp minor, $^2/_4$), and though here, as in the Sextet, op. 48, it takes the place of the usual slow movement, there is not lacking the lively and spirited dance-paragraph so character-

istic of the Dumka. The form of the movement is a three-part rondo
(*a b c a b a*), with a quick section in the middle (*c*), while both the
outer paragraphs are themselves symmetrically three-part (*a b a*).
Their principal song theme (3), with its tone of retrospective lament
embellished by a lovely counterpoint:

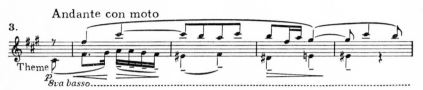

is set within the refrain-like framework of a four-bar motif:

which gives the whole motive its specifically ballad character. Then
as if lighting up the sad cast of countenance with a sunny smile
there arises, in a dialogue between the two violins, the fascinatingly
beautiful line of the secondary theme:

Very soon, however, this gleam of sunshine vanishes, for the development of the above-quoted theme 5, in which triplets are substi-
tuted for the semiquaver element, returns to the mood of pensive
longing which, with the re-entry at the end of the paragraph of the
principal theme (3), also recaptures its mood.

The middle section of the Dumka is a quick *Vivace* of which the
vigorous theme is derived from motif 4, the ballad-like refrain to
the principal theme:

4a.   Vivace

Skipping from one instrument to another, this theme sets the whole movement dancing to the irresistable rhythms of a dance which reaches a climax when the viola and violoncello storm in with the theme in octaves (F sharp major). Thereupon a sudden chord of the sixth in G major cuts short the whirling motion, theme 4 providing the transition to the third part, which is an almost literal repetition of the first, but rescored and so in a new sound colouring.

The third Scherzo movement (*Molto vivace*, A major, ³/₄) is designated Furiant. In its rhythmic substance it is not pure furiant in form, lacking the typical alternation of triple and duple time and keeping exclusively instead, as in the Sextet, op. 48, to a triple-time dance rhythm of great verve and unmistakable Slavonic colouring. The opening section, gay and sunny, is built up of three themes expressively well contrasted. The first is overflowing with rhythmic invention and the expression of unclouded good spirits and joy of living.

6.   Molto vivace

The second is slower in pace and is not, in its gently undulating motion, altogether without a touch of yearning:

7.

The last of the group of three themes is Slavonic in the softness of its line and its equally typical harmonic simplicity:

8.

but it is enlivened by the merry concluding strain of the first theme
(6), which also brightens up the middle section of the Furiant whose
mood is very much calmer and somewhat dreamy, its theme being
tinged with a tender Russian melancholy:

9.   Poco tranquillo

The third part of the Furiant is a substantially shortened repetition
of the first and again in new harmonic colouring further enriched
by a wealth of contrapuntal embroidery of the individual themes.

The fourth movement *(Allegro,* A major, $^2/_4$) is dominated
almost throughout by a mood of unperturbed good spirits. It is a
bustling finale in sonata form, rhythmically very lively and with
gay and delightfully fresh counterpoints. Its principal theme is composed of a small, perky little phrase (10*a*) and of a broad gaily
chattering period (10*b*), both figures being later attributed an important role in the thematic design:

10 a.   Allegro

10 b.

After a transition in which the opening rhythmic unit from 10*b* is
given considerable prominence, the subordinate theme is introduced—reminiscent in shape of themes from the "Slavonic" period
of Dvořák's production, with which it also has in common the
typical close into the relative minor mode:

11.

The exposition of the themes closes with a rhythmically proud and sprightly motif (12). This forms the transition to the syncopated closing theme (13), emotionally melting, calm and accompanied by an independent counterpoint in the violin:

12.

13.

The development is distinguished by the refinement of the contrapuntal embroidery and draws exclusively for its material on the two parts of the main theme (10a, 10b), of which especially the second is handled with great harmonic skill (a lovely effect is achieved by the emotionally coloured augmentation in the minor), and which serve also for the working out of a charming little fugato. The principal theme having thus been thoroughly exploited in the development, the composer omits it at the beginning of the recapitulation, returning to it only in the coda which concludes the whole work in a wildly happy whirl of semiquavers.

III

COMPOSITIONS FOR FOUR INSTRUMENTS

A. QUARTETS FOR STRINGS

QUARTET IN A MAJOR
for two violins, viola and violoncello. — Opus 2.

Written in the first quarter of 1862 (at the end of the score manuscript is the remark: "Thanks be to God! Composed in 1862, in March after the call-up of conscripts. Ant. Leop. Dvořák"); revised and abridged in 1887.—First performed by Karel Ondříček, Jan Pelikán, Petr Mareš and Alois Neruda at the eighth popular concert of the "Umělecká Beseda" on January 6th, 1888, in Prague. Published by the "Hudební matice Umělecké besedy", Prague, in 1948.—Duration: 29$^{1}/_{2}$ minutes.

The first of the group of Dvořák's fourteen quartets was written about eight months after the String Quintet, op. 1 (see page 28) as the artist's second serious composition. It was a work as full of promise for the future as the first, especially in the fertility and range of the musical content, the vitality and individual strokes of the compositional treatment and the unusually sound and colourful instrumentation. It is, indeed, in all respects a work of life's creative spring, of thoughts bubbling up from a deep and full source of innate musicality and composed with youthful élan and spontaneity, both in expression and design. It differs from the Quintet, op. 1, in having four movements and in the inclination to that lack of economy and balance in the handling of the thematic material which reached its extreme limit about the seventies (Dvořák's later revision made extensive cuts in the first, second and last movements). Both in mood and expression, the Quartet bears clear traces of the influence of the Neo-Romanticists. In several features of the work, however, there are recognizable, at the same time, undeniable intimations of the composer's maturing personality.

The first movement opens with a slow introduction *(Andante,* A major, $^8/_8$), to which the composer returns at the very end of the finale. Here is its beginning:

1.   Andante

The opening interval of the major second, E—F sharp, is the element from which the principal theme of the quick part is then developed *Allegro*, A major, $^6/_8$) and which steps out with charming freshness and vigour.

2.   Allegro

Its mood is maintained in the more smoothly phrased subordinate theme:

3.

and is intensified in the robust rhythms of the final theme:

4.

The development, restless in its modulations, works up very freely elements of the above-quoted themes, presenting them in ever new variants and new figurations as also in the recapitulation which brings the movement to a calm close.

The second movement *(Adagio,* F sharp minor, $^3/_4$) may be described as two-part, the second part being an abridged replica of the first. Introduced by several bars of grave, long-sustained chords, it grows out of two basic themes. Of these the first begins with a calm melodious thought of large compass which, after eight bars, is followed by a strain of deeply passionate fervency:

In relation to Dvořák's later slow movements, this Adagio is like a half-open bud as compared with the glory of the flower in full bloom. It has not yet their intoxicating fragrance and maturity, yet is able to delight the listener with the charm and purity of its lyrical feeling.

The third movement *(Allegro scherzando,* A major, $^3/_4$) is Dvořák's first and already fairly characteristic scherzo. It is composed in ternary form, both its symmetrical outer parts and the Trio being themselves three-part, and with independent thematic ideas for the middle paragraph. In the symmetrical parts the quieter first theme (7) contrasts with the livelier rhythmic structure of the second (8):

7. Allegro scherzando

8.

The Trio, set in the key of F sharp minor, has as its principal theme a typical dance motif alternating triple and duple time:

9.

while the theme of the middle paragraph consists of light sweeping arpeggio figures over a calmly undulating accompaniment by the rest of the ensemble:

10.

In this movement, too, there is discernible the germ out of which Dvořák's delightfully attractive later Scherzos were to develop.

The fourth movement *(Allegro animato*, A major, $^4/_4$) returns to the mood of youthful vitality and the sonata form of the first movement. It steps out boldly with a lively energetic principal theme, the first two notes reminiscent of the two opening themes in the first movement (1 and 2):

11. Allegro animato

In the episodic section this theme is followed by two transitional themes:

A contrast of expression is provided by the subordinate theme:

and this expression continues in its subsequent combination with triplets and semiquaver figurations till it is interrupted by the sforzando chords of the simple concluding theme:

In the fairly broad development, the figures of the various themes reappear in a luxuriance of imitations and variations forming the harmonic stream which runs its course through a wide range of key. A number of surprisingly bold modulations distinguish the recapitulation, which omits only the episodic motif 12a of the above-quoted themes, while a no less surprising stroke is the way in which the dynamic build-up of the final theme is cut short by the unexpected but quite logically interpolated grave theme of the slow introduction to the first movement (1). Then once again the vigorous principal theme (11) makes a short reappearance, dying away at the conclusion of the composition in a quiet, high-pitched and delicate A major chord.

QUARTET IN F MINOR
for two violins, viola and violoncello.

Written between September and October 4th, 1873.—First performed at the first independent concert of the Kramář Quartet (Jan Buchtele, Ferdinand Kahánek, J. Lupínek and Václav Kefurt) on January 11th, 1930, in the hall of the Prague Corn Exchange.—Published by Breitkopf & Härtel, 1929.—Duration: 32—35 minutes.

The first step on the road leading out of the most critical stage of Dvořák's struggle for mastery of the cyclic sonata form was in his chamber music composition, the Piano Quintet in A major written in 1872 (see p. 45), while the next step was the pair of string quartets composed a year later and in close succession. In neither of these compositions, of which the first is in the key of F minor and the second in A minor, did Dvořák succeed in overcoming the rambling presentation and development of the thematic material, which is especially marked in the sonata movements (the first movement of the F minor Quartet still contains over 620 bars!) and which characterized the earlier quartets. Yet here a decided advance is apparent, similar to that in the piano quintet, in respect of the themes themselves, which are much more expressively concentrated and regular, besides being well contrasted, so that the movement assumes as a result greater clarity, coherence and plasticity of form. The two quartets show distinct progress also in the frequent glimpses they give of the well-defined features of the composer's individual and specifically Czech creative personality. In content they are interesting as dating from the period of Dvořák's marriage to Anna Čermáková and represent the composer's reckoning up with his unquiet past and also the reflection of moments of sweet bliss auguring a happier future.

The Quartet in F minor, which alone of the two has survived complete and been both published and performed—but only a full quarter of a century after the composer's death (in the revised version of the German composer, Günther Raphael)—is in four movements and in content preceeds from the still very grave and overcast mood of the opening movement to an unaffectedly gay and happy conclusion. It is as if the composer wanted, on the threshold of a new and brighter phase of his life, first to look back at the past so full of material hardships and at his difficult artistic beginnings, and to recapitulate the course of his life, its sunlight and its shadows, and only then, at the joyful close, to greet the new life with its promise of family happiness and artistic success along the path towards full maturity of musical expression.

The first movement (*Allegro* in the manuscript, in the published edition *Moderato* and then *Allegro con brio*, F minor, ³/₄) is passionately agitated throughout with moments of stubborn defiance or of softly yearning desire, while the harmonies are predominantly dark in colouring. The mood of the movement is clearly suggested from the first in the principal theme, of which especially the introductory pair of bars is the dominating element in the whole structure. It enters straight away in the second violin and violoncello in unison, the viola joining them in the fifth bar and providing the middle harmonies:

1.   Allegro

The theme is discussed at considerable length, important structural accessories being an animated triplet figure:

2.

and then comes a quieter transitional motif (3), out of the first bars of which there develops the clear but nonetheless emotionally coloured subordinate theme (4):

3.

4.

5.

The thematic material of the movement is completed with the cadence theme, which is of a more lively dance character and shows
a predilection for alternating triple and duple time:

A very long development, scarcely perceptibly marked off from
the exposition, presents a variety of changing moods, now bustling
and animated, now more tranquil, and deals with most of the above-
quoted themes. A new and further development of the themes comprises the content of the recapitulation, which is also broadly discursive. Diverging from the exposition in its omission of the cadence
theme (5), the movement finishes with a terse, dynamically agitated
coda in the bright key of F major.

The second movement *(Andantino con moto quasi allegretto,*
F minor, $^6/_8$) is a calm and very intimate song tinged with a sweetly
contemplative melancholy. In form it is a small-scale rondo based

on the scheme *a b a c a b a*, of which the main feature is the simple,
charmingly lyrical and relatively tranquil principal theme *(a)*:

6.   Andantino quasi allegretto

which, in the outer sections of the movement, alternates with a
slightly rocking motif 6*b* whose characteristic figure provides elsewhere, too, in the movement an important element in contrapuntal
accompaniments:

7.   Vl. I.

the middle part of the movement *(c)* on the other hand, grows out
of thoughts pointing to the close vicinity of the E flat major Symphony:

8.

The movement has neither the breadth nor the depth of Dvořák's
great Adagios but can certainly bear comparison with them in
melodic charm and truthfulness of emotion (reference is made to
its adaptation in the "Romance" for Violin with orchestral or piano
accompaniment op. 11 at the end of this analysis).

The third movement, the Scherzo, is not complete. In the
manuscript score, there is the beginning of the introductory part,
then the Trio and the third part, considerably abridged as compared
with the first; missing, however, is the expositional part of the first
section preceding the Trio; in all, according to the pagination, four
pages (in the published score, the Trio rightly follows the fragment
of the preceding part without any attempt at reconstruction). The

outer parts of the Scherzo have the character of a waltz slightly tinged with melancholy and somewhat reminiscent of Chopin *(Tempo di valse*, F minor, $^3/_4$*/)*, its melodic line developing sequentially out of this motif:

9.   Tempo di Valse

A lively contrast to this walz section, both in mood and expression, is the middle part (Trio, *Allegretto*, F major, $^2/_4$). This is due not only to the brightness of the major key and the vigorous march rhythm, but also to the Czech national tone of the theme and the purely Dvořák invention of its treatment. Here is the theme:

10.

The whole of this trio section, which, as regards content and structure, is an interesting anticipation of the Scherzo Trio in the C major quartet, op. 61, composed eight years later (see Ex. 9, p. 94) is delightfully fresh and Czech in feeling, nor is the impression dispelled by the short return to the yearning Waltz part of the introduction.

This impression is, on the contrary, further confirmed by the fourth movement of the quartet *(Allegro molto*, F minor, $^2/_4$) which drives away the last traces of the author's melancholy and greets with jubilation a new and happier life. Written in sonata form, the beginning and the disposition of the thematic material are of special interest. The first thirty-three bars comprise what is actually a modulating transition from the dominant seventh chord in the key of G flat major to the tonic key of F minor, in which the

rôle of principal theme is assumed by the restless rising triplet figure
which is really an inversion of the analogous figure (2) in the first
movement:

11.   Allegro molto

The return to the tonic marks the signal for the entry of a second
principal theme which, in contrast to the first, has a melting melodic line and a typical Dumka colouring:*

12.

The restlessness of the introductory part reappears with figure 11,
this time developed with greater dynamic energy, whereupon the
violins in the higher register deliver the lively subordinate theme,
which in its whole character, (syncopated rhythms, alternating
major and minor, sudden shifts of key) seems to belong altogether
to the period of the "Slavonic Dances":

13.

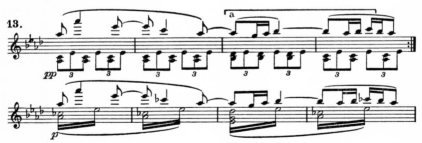

* Its relationship to the theme of the second of the "Slavonic Dances", op.
46, is obvious:

This theme, with which the composer appears to greet the new life, rich in happy and fruitful work in the service of national art, also provides the main thematic core of the development, and is extraordinarily varied in its modulations and moods. If the second, lyrically meditative part of the principal theme (12) is not heard here, it is given ample opportunity to display itself, with a wealth of harmonic embroidery, in the otherwise regular recapitulation (not excepting the tonal character of the themes) which winds up with a gay, high-spirited dance, in general character as well as instrumentation, completely Dvořák.

Proof that Dvořák himself did not intend this quartet any more than the following one in A minor for publication is the fact that quite soon after its composition (not later that 1877), he worked up the slow movement into a new quite independent work for violin and small orchestra which he entitled "Romance" and had published by Simrock in 1879, as op. 11. The Romance is designed on a fairly broad scale in sonata form (*Andante con moto*, F minor, $^{6}/_{8}$), the scheme being as follows:

The composition begins with a delicate orchestral introduction developed canonically from the principal theme of the quartet movement (6) which, here, too, retains the leading rôle. There follows the first movement proper, which literally reproduces the opening twenty-seven bars from the quartet movement. After a transitional passage of several bars, an altogether new and beautifully vocal theme makes its entry in the key of E major, recalling melodically and harmonically (but especially in its scheme of modulations) the composer's Wagnerian fever of a phase successfully outgrown:

The whole exposition concludes with a new softly insinuating final theme, as delicate as it is charming:

An orchestral tutti based on this theme now leads to a new short development, followed by a recapitulation working up the subordinate and final themes in the signature key of F major.

Thus arose a composition very effectively written for the instrument, very refined in its thought-content and of truly ethereal delicacy of expression and tone colouring (the orchestra comprises in addition to the strings, a pair each of flutes, oboes, clarinets bassons and horns).

QUARTET IN A MINOR
for two violins, viola, and violoncello. — Opus 16.

Begun in the middle of September 1874, the second movement completed on the 17th, the third on the 21st and the fourth on the 24th of the same month.—Dedicated to Dr Ludevít Procházka.—First performed at a meeting of the "Circle of Young Musicians" on June 17th, 1875, and publicly at a concert of the "Society for Chamber Music" in Prague, on the 29th December, 1878, the performers being Antonín Bennewitz, Eduard Wittich, Vilém Bauer and Bruno Wilfert.—Published in parts by Emanuel Starý, Prague, in 1875, and in score and parts by Bote & Bock, Berlin, in 1893.—Duration: $23^{1}/_{2}$ minutes.

The Quartet in A minor, op. 16, is the first chamber music work from the period of Dvořák's creative development to be marked by complete clarification of the preceding process of strong formal fermentation and rapid advance towards formal simplification and concentration and artistic independence of expression. In the Quartet, op. 16, the striving after clarity, neatness and correctness of form is reflected in an almost exaggerated care and preciseness, so that not only is the prodigality of musical thought of the preceding quartet limited in each movement to two independent themes, but the function of each is substantially simplified by the avoidance of any form of melodic or contrapuntal combination. Thus there arose a work, refined in thought and sensitive in feeling, a work carefully designed and carried out, testifying to a notable advance towards purity of style. In spite of some unusual strokes (such as the harmonic plan of the last movement), this is a work inspired by a more straightforward and somehow more close-knit creative and compositional fantasy than is to be found in a number of Dvořák's earlier chamber works, and which is an inseparable feature of all his later works. Perhaps this is in part due to the character of the content which, with its setting in a minor key, points to a mood inwardly gloomy and in places almost bordering on spiritual anguish, and only in the last movement breaking through to an expression of manly resolve.

The first movement *(Allegro ma non troppo,* A minor, ³/₄) is written in regular and simple sonata form with a single pair of themes. The principal theme, in line and rhythm softly undulating:

1. Allegro ma non troppo

defines the basic mood of the movement all the more effectually as it is the only thematic element made use of in the fairly extensive development in which, however, it at times assumes a hard stubbornness of expression. The second and subordinate theme, which appears only in the exposition and in the recapitulation, is, as compared with the first, somewhat more flexible as well as clearer and more animated in expression:

The second movement *(Andante cantabile,* F major, $^4/_4$), borne on a broad and calm melodic stream, is in regular three-part rondo form. The theme of the outer parts, to which the interval of a descending minor seventh gives a special quality, develops a gravely beautiful melodic line, the second element of which (indicated by a bracket) has an interesting similarity to the final figure of the principal theme of the first movement (1):

The core of the middle part of the movement, which is broadly worked out, is a choral-like theme whose monotonous rhythm colours the whole section:

With a quotation of this theme, after a return to a somewhat modified version of the first part, the movement closes in grave and dignified mood.

The third movement *(Allegro scherzando,* A minor, $^3/_2$) keeps to the simplest form of the classical scherzo with the character of a quick minuet. The outer, identical sections grow from a lively hopping theme and, despite the minor key, are in smiling mood and quite ready to be gay:

5. Allegro scherzando

The theme of the Trio, which is in the key of C major, has by contrast a calmer and more sober melodic line:

6.

and so provides the necessary contrast in mood to that of the Scherzo.

The fourth movement *(Allegro ma non troppo,* A minor, $^2/_2$), formally the freest in construction of the whole quartet, concludes the work in a tone of growing brightness and good spirits. Written in two-theme sonata form, it is not a little surprising in its almost complete avoidance of the signature key of A minor. Thus it opens with triplets full of excited anticipation in F major forming the background for the entry of a partly smooth and partly rhythmical skipping principal theme:

7. Allegro ma non troppo

If this theme at times diverges into the key of A minor, it is only in order to underline a mood of festive resolution. In general, however, the clear, warm tonality of A major prevails, in which key the diatonically constructed subordinate theme is presented for the first time:

8.

It also remains the dominant key for the whole development, working mainly with the subordinate theme (8) and the triplet base of the principal theme (7). The recapitulation opens with the principal theme still in F major, but very soon it, too, opens into A major in which both themes are worked up with a steady intensification of movement and tone till it reaches an almost hymn-like *grandioso* at the conclusion of the composition.

QUARTET IN E MAJOR

for two violins, viola and violoncello. — Opus 80 (originally 27).

The first movement was written in score between the 20th and the 25th, the second by the 28th, the third by the 29th of January and the fourth by the 4th of February, 1876.—First performed by the Joachim Quartet (Joachim, Hegemeister, Wirth and Diepert) at a concert held on December 29th, 1890 in Berlin, and in Prague by the Bohemian Quartet (Hoffmann, Suk, Nedbal, Berger) at their first independent concert on October 22nd, 1892.—Published by Simrock in 1888, under a new opus number.—Duration: 27$^1/_2$ minutes.

The E major quartet is the first in the series of Dvořák's best-known string quartets. In expression it is interwoven, as was also the earlier A minor Quartet, op. 16, with a number of clearly recognizable reminiscences of Beethoven and, indeed, the spirit of the great classical genius makes itself felt in not a few ways in this work; in contrast to the A minor quartet, however, the composer's musical imagination is in no way restricted or shackled by this kinship but blossoms freely into the manifestation of a spirit individually and nationally consolidated and creatively mature, both in the quality and refinement of the thought-content as well as in the resourcefulness and mastery with which he handled the thematic material and in the elegance of the form. The content of the quartet was to a great extent predetermined by the fact that the work arose shortly before the sketch for Stabat Mater, as one of the composer's most intimate manifestations, whose mood and expression bear the imprint of personal sorrow at the loss of his first children. In this connection it is significant that, although the quartet is designated as being in a major key and also conceived in a major tonality, the greater part of the work is in minor keys and that where it does reach a major key the expression is rather yearningly overcast than clear and happy.

The first movement, in sonata form *(Allegro,* E major, $^4/_4$) is based on two themes only, of which the first (1) melodically restricted in compass to a fourth and subdued in expression by the movement in crotchets is calm and almost dreamy, while the second, subordinate theme (2), though enlivened with pizzicato quavers alternately in the viola and violoncello, is suffused with so much melancholy, so much soft Slav sadness (and even where it jumps, in the inimitably Dvořák manner, into the relative major) that it suffices to colour the mood of the whole movement:

Structurally the first movement of the quartet has a number of interesting features. Thus, in the exposition, for instance, even before the actual entry of the subordinate theme (2) in the key of C sharp minor, there are a number of anticipations of the theme scattered through the fairly broad exposition of the principal theme, which then returns instead of a final theme. The whole development then works exclusively with this theme (1), presenting it in its original form and in a wide variety of diminutions and imitations. Finally

the recapitulation is broadened to include richly inventive treatment both of the subordinate theme as well as of the concluding
part which culminates before the close with the principal theme
ascending into the heights interwoven with the clear, high tones of
the ether.

The second movement *(Andante con motto,* A minor, $^3/_8$) is
completely plunged in melancholy meditation. It has not the usual
breadth of Dvořák's Adagios, nor yet their depth of expression but,
as in the slow movement of the preceding symphony in F major,
is a kind of presage of the composer's later Dumka movements,
having the character of an intimate, unusually sensitive and, in its
Slav mournfulness, softly glowing song of two themes in rondo
form (3, 4). Of these only the second is capable of greater emotional
tension and this is then made full use of in the middle part and later
in the passage where it combines in counterpoint with the first
theme:

Nor does even the third, scherzo, movement *(Allegro scherzando,* E major, $^3/_4$) introduces any strongly contrasting nuances into
the basic mood of the work. In the outer parts of the regular ternary
scheme, the waltz theme, alternating triple and duple time, is
tinged with a Chopinesque romanticism:

The key signature of E major really only masks the key of C sharp minor. It is also the key in which the middle part of the scherzo is set and of the principal theme, which is rhythmically and melodically dynamic in character:

In its third paragraph there are intonations of a kind indicating that even the Scherzo of this work might be happier than it is. The visionary meditativeness of its conclusion only confirms this impression.

The last movement *(Allegro con brio,* E major, ⁴/₄) has undoubtedly more movement and decision, but otherwise it cannot be said that it gives to the conclusion of the work a brighter tone. This is apparent from the very beginning in the unorthodox tonality of G sharp minor (!) in which the first principal theme sadly delivers its lament in the viola as an inner part below agitated triplets in the violins and above the descending steps of the bass:

Not till bar 32 does the melodic stream swerve into the fundamental key of E major with a new theme, this time very resolute but already seeking in its second bar a close in C sharp minor.

More conciliatory but not without an undertone of passionate desire, the quieter subordinate theme is assimilated into the mood of the movement:

In the development, however, which works with all the above-quoted themes, outbursts of grief again appear, especially when the rhythm of the principal theme (7) takes over the canonically followed octaves of the violins and the two lower instruments. And also in the recapitulation, which sets in with the return to the second theme 8, quieter moods alternate with new outbursts right to the very conclusion, whereupon, after a last swing-back in the second last bar to C sharp minor, a resolutely struck dominant seventh chord finally carries the movement into the home tonic.

QUARTET IN D MINOR
for two violins, viola and violoncello. — Opus 34.

Written in score between the 7th and 18th of December, 1877.—Dedicated to Johannes Brahms.—First performed at a concert of the Musical Section of the Umělecká Beseda in Prague on February 27th, 1882, by Ferdinand Lachner, Petr Mareš, Václav Borecký and Alois Neruda.—Published by Schlesinger, Berlin, in 1880.—Duration: 29 minutes.

The character and quality of the Quartet in D minor were largely determined by two important circumstances. It arose closely following the completion of the score of Stabat Mater and also shortly after Dvořák had suffered the loss, within two months, of his first-born son and his second daughter. It took the form, therefore, of a very intimate, introspective spiritual confession of a soul deeply wounded by these blows of fate and so, in its content, there prevails the expression of reserved melancholy and meditative self-questioning. But it also arose only a few months before the first series of "Slavonic Dances", and not only does it approach closely in expression to the so-called "Slavonic" period of the composer's creation but it is, at the same time, a work with all the marks of the compositional mastery to which Dvořák had by this time fought his way. In the first connection, the Quartet is interesting as being the first instance in Dvořák's cyclic compositions of the introduction of an art stylisation of a folk dance (polka and sousedská) in the scherzo movement, while in the second, in addition to several typical Schubertisms, for the way in which the stylistic purity and ingenuity of the thematic treatment betrays the influence of Johannes Brahms, whose personal acquaintance Dvořák made at this time and to whom he also dedicated the work.*

In the first movement *(Allegro*, D minor, ³/₄), the prevailing tone of the meditative withdrawal of a deeply passionate spirit determined the character of the principal theme with which the movement opens. Gently, almost timidly, it is drawn over an accompaniment of undulating quavers in the principal key of D minor (2 a), brightening only temporarily in its further course into the key of G major (1 b):

------

* On Brahms's advice Dvořák changed a number of places in the quartet, as witness his letter to the German master of the 15th October 1879 in which he writes: "During your last stay in Prague you were so kind as to draw my attention to a number of things in my works and I must be very grateful to you for doing so as I really then found many bad notes which I have put right.

I felt myself all the more under the obligation, especially in the D minor Quartet, to change many things, since you were good enough to accept the dedication of the work; and thus it was my sacred duty to present to so great a master a work which conforms, if not in every respect, at least (forgive my lack of modesty) in many, to the demands which may be made on a work of art."

The third bar of the principal theme (bracketed in the example) is important as being the core out of which the other themes are built up. Out of its diminution there develops first a transitional theme, in canonic imitation, which with its sharp rhythmic accents for a while disturbs the expression between the first two-fold development of the principal theme.

The same thematic element in its original form is the germ out of which is developed the increasingly ardent and nationally coloured subordinate theme.

And the same element, accompanied by triplet figures, also forms a kind of final theme:

in as far as it may not be looked upon as merely a continuation of the broadly worked out subordinate theme which, after building up to a climax through a series of resolute chords, brings the climax to a delicate close.

A relatively short development, making use of the principal (1 a) and the subordinate theme (3), as well as the characteristic triplet figure from theme 4, maintains the basic mood of the movement except in several rather more agitated places. So also does the recapitulation which differs from the exposition only in the omission, at the beginning, of the transitional theme 2 with which it then opens the coda. The whirling waltz based on the principal theme at the conclusion and the decisive closing of the movement with the triplet figure only underlines the expression of spiritual anguish indicated by the yearning melancholy of the preceding part.

The second movement (Alla Polka, *Allegretto scherzando*) is designed as a scherzo—a scherzo idealizing, as in Smetana's Quartet "From My Life", Czech folk dance. The mood which it introduces into the quartet is, however, by no means particularly happy. The polka theme of the outer parallel parts (B flat major, $^2/_4$) begins in B flat major and in places marks out a more lively hopping rhythm, but not even this theme is without a suggestion of underlying pain, especially when its closing phrase turns into G minor or when at the close of the part, and also at the close of the movement, it slows down its pace as if lost in thought and fades into silence:

The Trio of the movement *(Quasi l'istesso tempo,* E flat major, $^3/_8$) only changes the key and rhythm without disturbing the yearning heartache of the outer parts. Its core is a meltingly melodic theme (6) whose ground bass at times becomes the leading melody either in the form of a variant (6a) or in its original form:

3. Letter from Johannes Brahms to Dvořák,
dated October 1879 (page 1)

4. Letter from Johannes Brahms to Dvořák,
dated October 1879 (page 2)

The third movement (*Adagio*, D major, $^3/_4$), broadly laid out,
is melodically one of the loveliest, in feeling among the deepest, and
in thematic treatment one of the richest of Dvořák's slow movements. In content it is a quietly ardent meditation, at times soaring
as it were in supplication to higher spheres, at times lost in sorrowful meditation, as it passes from the tonic key of D major to its relative minor. The muted strings effectively underline the delicacy
and intimacy of the mood and expression. The principal theme on
which the movement is based is an outwardly calm but inwardly
ardent and expressive theme, appearing at first in the form of a
canon between the violins together with the viola and the 'cello:

The figure in brackets then develops into a subordinate theme which
is treated at considerable length:

while the principal theme, now resumed in the viola, combines
with a countermelody in the higher registers of the first violin to
the accompaniment of the delicate shimmering of the demisemi-
quavers and expressive quaver pizzicatos, to form the amazingly
beautiful middle part of the movement, as if on a clear night there

should rise above the peacefully slumbering earth a song as up-
liftingly beautiful as it is sad:

The pizzicato quavers already referred to are a typical feature of
the movement, especially in the deep tones of the 'cello, right to its
close when, like a recollection of something dear that has vanished,
there suddenly rises a delicate quotation of the subordinate theme
from the first movement (3).

It is left to the last movement *(Poco allegro,* D minor, $^6/_8$) to
introduce into the work a new feeling of bustle and animation, but
not even here is there any question of inner clarification or brightening of mood. Hard and unconciliatory are the sharp rhythms of
the principal theme (8) and with a wild restlessness the waves of
thought rise and fall (9), while the subordinate theme expresses
deep yearning. (10):

And all these themes, springing clearly from a soul bruised and
suffering, determine the mood of the whole movement, which is
firmly and expressively designed, possessing an abundance of richly

varied imitation with a relatively concise development and recapitulation section and concluding in accelerated pace with a condensed quotation of all three themes.

QUARTET IN E FLAT MAJOR
for two violins, viola and violoncello. — Opus 51.

Written in score between December 25th 1878, and March 28th, 1879.—Dedicated to Jean Becker.—First performed at a private chamber music evening of the Joachim Quartet (Joachim, Hegemeister, Wirth, Diepert) on July 29th 1879, in Berlin.—Published by Simrock, Berlin, 1879.—Duration: 30 minutes.

The String Quartet in E flat major was composed at the request of the leader of the formerly famous Florentine Quartet, Jean Becker, who asked Dvořák to write for his ensemble a new "Slavonic Quartet". It was not difficult for Dvořák to grant this request as it came shortly after he had made a name for himself in the world with his "Slavonic Dances" and "Slavonic Rhapsodies", and when his art already bore the hallmark of personal and national individuality besides reflecting the striving to imbue the musical thought and mood of his compositions with the spirit of Czech folk music. He thus created a work which is not only a very intimate expression of his spirit, simple and manly in its humanity and at the same time of the utmost refinement and with a wide and finely differentiated range of mood, but which, for the beauty of its musical content and the masterly craftsmanship of the composition, is not only among the best works to come from his pen, but among the best in the whole literature of chamber music. The Slavonic character of the Quartet is emphasized by the circumstance that the Scherzo movement is designed as, and given the designation of, a Dumka, and that the last movement is an art stylization of the very characteristic Czech "skočná". An important key to the character of the thought-content of the E flat major Quartet is the fact of its being written at a time when a new and happy phase had set in both in Dvořák's family life and in his artistic career.

The first movement *(Allegro ma non troppo*, E flat major, $^4/_4$) indicates straight away the inwardly serene expression of the whole work with its frequent gleams of smiling humour, in the character of the principal theme, which, otherwise sweetly tender in its remarkable development from a tonic triad, is shot through at its conclusion with a roguish smile where its rhythm is enlivened by figure *a*:

This figure *a* also occurs elsewhere in the movement, strengthening its hearty, good-humoured character. Thus we come across it in the transitional thought (1*a*) which follows the first exposition of the principal theme and the fresh, carefree vigour with which it steps out prepares for the entry of the subordinate theme (2) and here we meet it again dancing above it:*

In the same way, in a variational form, it provides the contrapuntal embroidery for a new accessory motif:

* Compare the identical rhythmic figure in the polka theme of the scherzo movement of the Piano Trio in B flat major, op. 21, example 6. p. 148.

The development works mainly with the principal theme (1), both in its original form and in its graver augmentations, agitated by allusions to the subordinate theme, as well as in the rhythmically firmer imitation of the transitional theme 1 a, and with any amount of delightfully spontaneous contrapuntal invention. An interesting point to note about the recapitulation is the way it opens with the subordinate theme, whereas the principal theme, along with motif 1 a, is used to build up the coda for which it also provides the delicate conclusion.

The second movement, entitled "Dumka", is written in a kind of rondo form in two parts strongly contrasted in mood in which the principal theme is created from the same thematic core, while both secondary themes are independent. In the first part (*Andante con moto*, G minor, $^2/_4$), the wistful principal theme is always drawn over an accompaniment of calm harp-like pizzicato chords, weaving a rhapsodically overlapping dialogue between violins and viola or between the two violins:

The second theme sounds like a tender lullaby over a delicately sinuous accompaniment:

In the second part *(Vivace,* G major, $^3/_8$) an ingenious variant of the principal Dumka theme is worked up into a gay, high-spirited dance of furiant character, purely Czech in tone colouring, rhythm and mood.

3*a.* **Vivace**

In the middle yet a new theme appears presented by the 'cello, its syncopated rhythm giving the impression of duple time:

5.

Both parts are repeated, with the difference that the quick part *(Presto)* remains in the tonic key of G minor, which somewhat modifies its expression. The characteristic rhythm of figure *a* from the first movement is also made skilful use of in the Dumka.

The third movement, bearing the title "Romance" *(Andante con moto,* B flat major, $^2/_8$), is of relatively small dimensions but in expression a wonderfully ardent and at the same time wistfully dream-like nocturne. It grows out of a single theme (6), as the second more serious thought (6a) is really only a derivative of the first.

6.   **Andante con moto**

This movement is, indeed, one of the pearls of Dvořák's intimate lyrics, a movement of bewitching variety of mood, whose expressive and formal transparency reflects all the more clearly the composer's fertility of invention and mastery of the compositional art.

The fourth movement of the Quartet *(Allegro assai,* E flat major, $^2/_4$) has aptly been described as a pure Czech "skočná" in sonata form. Its mood intensifies still further the gaiety of the opening movement. Its principal theme has a high-spirited carefree character: it starts off with a group of gay semiquavers, stamps out a defiant syncopation in the second bar and finishes off in the last two bars with a *furiant*-like gesture:

The closing cadence of the theme, as so frequently in this phase of Dvořák's creation, modulates into the relative minor without, however, affecting the basic mood which is intensified rather than otherwise when two independent countermelodies are added to the theme:

A sense of humour is apparent in the first transitional thought:

and also in the way the motif, at first bluff and hearty, is unexpectedly repeated in quiet octaves. And still more pawky is the
humour of the accessory motif in two-voice combination sung with
an air of happy nonchalance by the two violins to the pizzicato
accompaniment of the 'cello:

The subordinate theme has at first a slight touch of melancholy
about it:

but the deviation in mood is only temporary, for this theme, too,
can be jolly as soon as it brightens into the major mode or is under-
propped by sharp rhythmic accents. A constructionally interesting
detail is that, on the début of this theme, the first violin weaves
about it a melody clearly related to the principal theme of the first
movement (1).

The exposition of the subordinate theme goes over imperceptibly
into the development and is later joined by the principal theme.
The recapitulation is a considerable abridgment of the exposition,
both accessory motifs being omitted, the second, however, appearing at the very close when it winds up the work with an expression
of boisterous high spirits.

QUARTET IN C MAJOR

for two violins, viola and violoncello. — Opus 61.

Written in score between October 25th and November 10th, 1881 (the second movement begun on the 27th, the third on the 29th of October and the fourth on the 4th of November).—Dedicated to Court Kapellmeister Josef Hellmesberger.—First perfomed on December 6th, 1882, in Bonn; in Prague, on January 3rd, 1884, at a chamber music evening of the Umělecká Beseda (Ferdinand Lachner, Raušer, Josef Krehan, Alois Neruda comprising the quartet).—Published by Simrock in February 1882.—Duration: 35 minutes.

Just as the previous quartet in E flat major was written at the request of Jean Becker, leader of the Florentine quartet, so also the quartet in C major was the fulfilment of a promise made, in the autumn of 1881, to the leader of the famous Viennese Quartet, Court Kapellmeister Josef Hellmesberger senior, in reply to a similar request. Indeed, Dvořák was compelled this time to fulfil his promise with the greatest celerity as Hellmesberger announced the date of the performance of the new work even before Dvořák had put pen to paper. And Dvořák did make all haste, interrupting, though unwillingly, his work on the sketch of the opera Dimitri, which he had been engaged upon since the beginning of the preceding month of April. This is clear from a letter to Alois Göbl at Sychrov near Turnov, dated the 5th November, 1881, in which he writes: "I see from the newspapers that Hellmesberger is going to play my new quartet, which I haven't even got yet, on the 15th December. What else could I do then than put aside the opera and start to write the quartet!" With what expedition he set to work is also clear from the fact that he began the quartet first of all in the key of F major, completing the score of the first movement in a mere three days (between the 7th and 9th of October at Vysoká), whereupon, evidently not satisfied with it, he rejected it and made a new start, this time choosing the key of C major for the new, definitive quartet, and completing the whole work, in sketch and in score, in a matter of less than four weeks.*

The work which thus took form may be described as the first characteristic example of that period in Dvořák's creative production in which the artist, in reaction to the preceding "Slavonic Period", very considerably loosened his close inventive affinities with the expression of Czech folk music. In the C major Quartet this was effected at the cost of a distinctly noticeable bias towards Beethoven classicism, but by no means at the cost of any falling-off in the refinement, spontaneity of strength of the composer's creative art. On the contrary, in the beauty, the expressiveness and the

* The rejected movement, written in sonata form, published by Hudební Matice, Prague, in 1949 worked mainly with these themes:

stylistic purity of the musical thought, in the resource with which the thematic material is handled and in the boldness of the design, this Quartet marks a new and significant advance in Dvořák's chamber music composition and a further highly convincing proof of his genius. It is a work of rare inner strength, of proud and mature manliness and, especially in the instrumental tone-colouring, of remarkable clarity.*

The clue to the character of the first movement of the quartet (*Allegro*, C major, $^4/_4$) is contained in the important principal theme comprising a group of three motifs based on the same rhythmic elements.

It is a theme of great beauty and intensity, manly and self-confident in expression, its melodic line as well as its rhythmic and harmonic

* It was evidently due to being pressed for time and his preoccupation with another large work (the opera "Dimitri") which led Dvořák, contrary to his habit, to make use in this Quartet of three older thematic ideas: for the beginning of the second movement, the original but later discarded sketch of the slow movement of the Violin Sonata, op. 57, from the preceding year, and, as the principal themes of the third and fourth movements, two motifs from the Polonaise for Violoncello and Piano, which he wrote in 1879 as a piece of occasional music not to be included in the body of his definitive works (published in 1926).

structure tinctured by the spirit of Beethoven, which also permeates
the subordinate theme, contrasting, however, with the former in its
calm movement and diffidence of expression:

The softly emotional concluding theme of the movement is the most
typically Dvořák, and also the most thoroughly Czech:

Whereas both the last-quoted themes, the subordinate and the concluding theme, are given a relatively short presentation, both in the
exposition and in the recapitulation, the structural nerve of the rest
of the movement is dominated by the principal theme, both as a
whole and in its part (especially the triplet figure I), which is given
ample room to display itself at the beginning of the exposition. This
provides the core of the development which is worked out with a
rich variety of contrapuntal devices and key modulations and—
with the exception of a short quotation of theme 2—also of the
splendidly impressive and spiritually clarified coda.

The second movement *(Poco adagio and molto cantabile,* F major,
$^4/_4$) is a calmly declaimed song, of deep fervency and unusual
melodic refinement. It opens with an intimate dialogue between
the violins over an accompaniment of undulating triplets in the
viola and violoncello:

Poco adagio e molto cantabile

After a short rather more animated passage modulating into D flat major, the song continues with a new theme, its veiled expression of melancholy underlined by an occassional wavering between the major and minor mode:

The prevailing mood of the movement is not affected even by another transitional modulating passage, taken up by each of the instruments in turn:

and leading into the last part of the movement, which makes further development of the first theme (4), alluding only quite shortly to the second theme (5) and finally bringing the movement to a dreamy close.

The third movement is a high-spirited three-part Scherzo, of which the completely corresponding outer parts *(Allegro vivo,* A minor, $^3/_4$) are all the more reminiscent of the Beethoven Scherzo by contrast with the strong personal and national individuality which distinguished the Scherzos in his preceding cyclic compositions. These sections are dynamic in movement and rhythmically sharply profiled, growing, on the one hand, out of the motif which, in a major variant, was originally the subordinate theme in the above-mentioned Violoncello Polonaise from the year 1879 (its kinship with the triplet element I in theme 1a of the first movement cannot, however, be overlooked):

and, on the other, out of the calmer episodic motif which twice
alternates with the lively contrapuntal play based on the preceding
principal theme:

If in the parallel parts thoughts of Beethoven are never far from
the mind, the middle part of this movement (*Trio, L'istesso tempo,*
A major, $^2/_4$) is, in the harmony and freshness of its musical thoughts,
as well as in its modulations and tone-colouring, much closer to
Schubert. But above all it is typically Dvořák, and decisively so in
the character of the two themes on which it is based and which
alternate according to the rondo scheme *a b a b a.* The first of these,
broadly developed (here the theme from the Trio of the Scherzo
movement in the F minor Quartet, 1873, comes to mind), is Dvořák
in the charm of its smilingly Czech melodic line and also in the
modulation of the close of its first period into the relative minor:

And no less typically Dvořák is the second theme, the playful dancing rhythms of its main line being charmingly set of by the lyrical
cantabile of the countermelody:

The last movement of the Quartet (Finale, *Vivace,* C major,
$^2/_4$) remains true to the basically Beethoven conception in as far as
the general character of its thought-content and the boldness of
conception of the sonata rondo form bears a certain resemblance to

the last movement of the first of the three Rasumovsky Quartets, op. 59, in F major. And it is just this movement that reflects most strongly the artistic personality of its author. This is apparent in the introductory principal theme, broadly and skilfully treated from the first and retaining its prominence throughout the movement:*

The flexible rhythms of this theme with its defiant accents and the way it hovers harmonically between C major and E minor are as Dvořák in character as are the wide stepping-stones in the melodic line and its softly melancholy expression.

Out of these central themes of very moderate dimensions there is built up a movement, spaciously planned, finely articulated and organically coherent, with innumerable strokes of genius in the inexhaustible variety of its thematic treatment, the prevailing happy tone of which mounts, at the conclusion, to a song of jubilation all the more effective for the powerful contrast presented just before the end by a profoundly lovely cadence in the first violin.

* Here is the melodic shape of the middle theme in three-four time of the Violoncello Polonaise from which it is derived.

QUARTET IN F MAJOR
for two violins, viola and violoncello. — Opus 96.

Written in sketch between the 8th and 10th of June, 1893, and in score as follows: the first movement between the 12th and the 15th, the second between the 15th and the 17th, the third by the 20th and the fourth between the 20th and the 23rd of the same month, all at Spillville in America.—First performed by the Kneisel Quartet (Frank Kneisel, Otto Roth, Louis Svecenski, Alwin Schroeder) at their concert on New Year's Day, 1894, in Boston. Published by Simrock in 1894.—Duration: 22 minutes.

The Quartet in F major was the first of a pair of compositions which Dvořák wrote in the summer of 1893 when on vacation, in the country town of Spillville in Iowa, during his appointment as Director of the National Conservatory in New York. (The second was the string Quintet in E flat major, op. 97, for which see p. 37). In order of time, Dvořák's Quartet followed immediately upon his famous "From the New World" Symphony, with which it has much in common not only as regards mood but especially also in the American features of the thematic ideas (the pentatonic scale, the lowered seventh degree in the minor scale, the dotted and syncopated rhythms etc.) and in the very clear, plastic and relatively simple formal design. It differs from the Symphony mainly in its greater conciseness both of expression and structure (it is by far the shortest of Dvořák's chamber compositions) and in the relatively much greater intimacy and simplicity of its emotional content.

In order fully to grasp the inner character of the Quartet it must be remembered that its composition was preceded by a sojourn of eight months in the bustle of the city life of New York, in a socially and nationally foreign environment in which Dvořák was not only the object of a great variety of celebrations and official honours but also of unpleasant sensation-mongering and journalists' disputes. The Quartet was therefore the first expression of the new impressions evoked by the abrupt and welcome change to the peace and quiet of a farming settlement in the heart of the country and to the society of a simple farming community of his fellow-countrymen. The mood of the outer movements of the Quartet, so surprisingly light-hearted and playful, smilingly gay and overflowing with high spirits or again expressing an idyllic calm—is a true reflection of Dvořák's inner life, of his spiritual experiences in the silence of the beauties of nature, with their peculiar and for him exotic character, in the circle of the simple but intelligent and shrewd Czech people, among respected farmers, companionable parish priests and dear old grannies who listened with tears in their eyes to the old church hymns of their native Czech villages played to them on the organ at Mass by their far-famed countryman. And so, if we picture to ourselves the composer lost in thought somewhere in the solitude of these great spaces, listening to the song of birds different from and yet reminding him of those in his beloved summer retreat at Vysoká in far-off Bohemia, then we can fully enter into the mood of the slow movement of the Quartet and that of the intimate little Scherzo.

"Thanks be to God! I am content. It went quickly" was the note Dvořák made below the last line of the sketch for this composition, and he had every reason to be content, not only because "it went quickly" (the sketch took him only three days, while the score was completed in sixteen) but because he had created a work which, despite its relative simplicity of aspect, bears the authentic hallmark of creative genius and holds an important place in his chamber music as a new and original work. This is due in part to the thought-content of the Quartet, along with the characteristic features of this period of Dvořák's creation referred to above (the lowered seventh degree is indicated in the example by the sign $\times$) and in part to the composer's lightness of touch and charmingly spontaneous handling of the musical material as well as to the intensely intimate, playful range of moods far removed from all stormy outbursts of feeling.

The first movement *(Allegro ma non troppo*, F major, $^4/_4$) runs its course in the mood generally described above. The smiling contentment of a bucolic existence illuminates the expression, which even when ruffled with sudden emotion immediately resumes its meditative tranquility. The principal say in the movement is given to the airy principal theme whose rhythmic variety is made good use of in the thematic embroidery:

In the introduction to the movement, with its rustling tremolo chord of F major in the violins, this theme is first presented by the viola and then repeated in the first violin. The closing figure of the theme, *(b)* provides the opportunity for the composer to develop it in a short transitional episode followed once more by the principal theme this time, however, only for the sake of effecting a rapid modulation to the key of the subordinate theme (A minor). The provenance of the new theme, constructed in two-part harmony, is clear not only from the minor seventh ($\times$):

but is also indicated by the pedal point in the viola and the hard pizzicato of a bare fifth in the violoncello. If the prevailing expression of the movement is thereby somewhat disturbed, complete tranquillisation sets in with the following delicate and wonderfully tender final theme which, melodically, is one of Dvořák's most delightful "American" motifs:

In the middle part of the movement, following on the exposition, which is repeated, considerable development is made especially of the principal theme (1), whose various figures serve to build up a varied but well-concentrated thematic mosaic. Only at the close of the development is a short canon worked out on an energetic theme, the second bar documenting its derivation from the subordinate theme (2):

The recapitulation diverges from the exposition only in that at the transition the violoncello sings, over an *ostinato* repetition of fragment *(b)* form theme 1, this new melodic variant of the final theme (3):

It is a typical Dvořák stroke, as is also the actual close of the movement, at first calmly and gravely ardent in tone, an agitated dialogue based on the elements *a* and *b* of the principal theme bringing it, then, to a very energetic conclusion.

The second movement *(Lento,* D minor, $^6/_8$) is one of the loveliest jewels among the song-form movements in Dvořák's chamber compositions. It is distinguished by the lyrical beauty of its melodic line, the emotional purity and depths of its expression and the peculiar charm of its pellucid harmonies, in which minor keys alternate with their relative or at least related major keys, no less than

by its natural flow and variety. It is a broadly designed song ema-
nating an inexpressible heartache beyond the reach of pain, of which
it might be said that it belonged to the family of Negro spirituals if
the two-part melody of the middle section were not sung in such
perfectly Czech thirds and sixths. Its melancholy expression is also
underlined by the monotonous ripple of the accompanying figure
over which the melodic line is drawn.

The thematic core of the movement is a calm eight-bar period, sung
first by the violin and then by the 'cello:

In its further course the first violin develops the figure from the
second last pair of bars of the preceding melody, the second violin
replying first with an independent countermelody:

and then combining with the leading part in a beautifully melodic
duet, which is typical of the whole middle part of the movement.
The duet increases in intensity of expression as it opens out into yet
another variant of the principal theme:

in which there sounds the wistful voice of an intimate longing and desire, but at the same time with more than a hint in its expression of rapturous inner happiness:

At the conclusion of the movement, melancholy again holds complete sway. Sadly plaintive in tone, the principal theme in the violoncello makes its way above the heavily measured pizzicato of the other instruments and, finally, over the mystic tremolo of the viola which closes the movement with a dolefully forlorn fall of a semitone.

The third movement *(Molto vivace,* F major, $^3/_4$) is a simple but delightful bagatelle built up from a single theme with a rhythmically vivacious opening clause and a gently rocking close.

Structurally the movement falls into two paragraphs which—in variational transformations—alternate *a b a b a.* The expression of the first paragraphs, which keeps to the key of F major, is characterized throughout by the skilful grouping of the rhythmic elements of the theme (mainly from its two even bars) and by the serenity of mood embodied especially in the independent variant in the high registers of the violins.*

The second paragraph is set in the key of F minor, its expression, in contrast to the first, being fantastically mysterious. In it an augmentation of the opening clause of the principal theme (5) passes like a *canto firmo* from one instrument to the next, interwoven now with one now with the other of two countermelodies:

These middle parts contribute most to the strongly exotic flavouring of the small-scale Scherzo, in which the economy of the thematic and modulating plan is fully balanced by the variety of rhythmic element and remarkably imaginative handling of the tone-colour combinations.

The fourth movement *(Vivace ma non troppo,* F major, $^2/_4$) concludes the Quartet with a very gay rondo *(a b a c a b a),* the char-

* According to a reminiscence of Josef Jan Kovařík, a native of Spillville and violinist who lived with Dvořák in New York and in Spillville, Dvořák divulged at the rehearsal of the F major Quartet that he had taken over this motif from the song of some exotic bird he had listened to on his rambles in the surroundings of Spillville:

acter of the mood being determined by the skipping rhythm of the
principal theme, which runs through almost the whole movement.
It appears in the very first bar of the second violin and viola,
encouraged by the light pizzicato of the 'cello, whereupon the first
violin takes it over and, in very leisurely but quite charming fashion,
prepares for the entry of the theme proper, which is made to wait
until bar thirty-three before being allowed its merry say.

Rhythmical, sharply accented chords, first in A minor and the
second time in C major, conclude each of the two introductory
statements of the theme spread over sixteen bars and, again, by a
purely Dvořák stroke, making the leap without any modulational
transition to A flat major in which, above the persistent hopping
movement of the principal theme, the violins declaim the broadly
vocal and ardently emotional subordinate theme to which occasional doubling in sixths and thirds gives a folk-music intonation:

After a new and high-spirited exposition of the principal theme
(6), the musical stream, having swerved into the tonality of D flat
major, suddenly becomes quieter in mood and movement. Pro-
ceeding by semitones and pianissimo, a short choral imitation is
worked out, as if someone were improvising delicately on the organ,
and a calm quotation of theme 6 leads into the last part of the movement, which concludes as with the parting hymn sung by a simple
and pious congregation (Meno mosso):

8.   Meno mosso

Perhaps the recollection of the early morning services at the Spill-ville church of St. Václav was here present to the composer's mind. But it is only a short, grave intermezzo in an otherwise happy and carefree movement, for, no sooner does the violoncello take over the pious theme from the violins in order to repeat it than the violins join in with a light figuration again shot through with the rhythm of the principal theme like the appearance of a merry twinkle in a pair of grave eyes. And soon this rhythm holds sway, a short dynamic climax paving the way for the sportive play of its own theme, one of many delightful and charming surprises being the shift of key from F major to D flat major. The entry of the subordinate theme (7) is this time at first somewhat wistful, but it soon clears up again, and, at the close of the movement, the principal theme has it all its own way, winding up the composition in a whirl of good spirits and jollity.

QUARTET IN A FLAT MAJOR
for two violins, viola and violoncello. — Opus 105.

The first movement begun on March 26th, 1895, in New York and completed after an interval of nine months in Prague where the other movements were then written: the second and third between the 19th and 25th of December and the fourth between the 26th and 30th of the same month in 1895.—First Prague performance by the Bohemian Quartet (Hoffmann, Suk, Nedbal, Wi-han) at a concert of the Czech Society for Chamber Music on January 21st, 1897. Previously performed in several towns in Germany and at a concert of the Dannreuther Quartet in New York. Published by Simrock in the summer of 1896.—Duration: 30 minutes.

Of the pair of string quartets with which Dvořák, on his return from a sojourn of three years in America, wound up not only his chamber music composition but that of his absolute music in general, the E flat major is actually the later, though it bears a lower opus number than the G major Quartet (op. 106). This is due to the fact that Dvořák began the Quartet in A flat major before departure for America, in the spring of 1895, correctly as his 105th work, but completed only the slow introduction and the expositional section of the first movement (as far as number four of the printed score). He did not resume work on it till the end of the same year at home, having previously created the G major Quartet which, in the manuscript score, is expressly described as "the first composition after my second return from America". He left the original opus numbers of the works, however, unchanged.

The Quartets are near each other not only by their close proximity in time, but also because their musical content grows out of the same feelings of inner happiness and content which filled the composer's soul at being at home again in his own beloved country and among his own people. And so, for the same reason, the musical expression has thrown off the characteristic traits of the preceding "American" period, the A flat major Quartet bearing in fact no trace of them. These two composition have yet one thing more in common: they are among the loveliest in thought and the most masterly in composition of Dvořák's chamber-music works. Both testify to his genius in the richness and originality of the inventive ideas and in the highly organised thematic handling and design. The classical form is the pattern on which this present Quartet is based, but only the middle movements conform closely to the scheme, while the other movements are, to a great extent, free, with remarkably bold and interesting structural divergencies.

The first movement of the Quartet in A flat major opens with a short introduction in slow tempo *(Adagio ma non troppo*, A flat minor, $^6/_8$) in which one instrument after another, from the lowest upwards, gravely presents the beginning of the principal theme (1a). A series of resolute chords interposes, and then a slow but ever brightening line of melody leads up to the Allegro part of the movement *(Allegro appasionato,* A flat major, $^4/_4$) setting off very effectively the happy vital challenge of the principal theme. Indeed, not inaptly, the beginning of this theme has been compared to a trumpet call. Its opening figure, which makes a fluttering leap from the tonic to the upper dominant, has something of an inspiring signal about it, not to battle—but rather to a rich feast of melodic thoughts:

Allegro appassionato

Not even the paragraph exposing the theme is content with its original form but straightway, over the rhythm of its last bar (bracketed in the example), introduces a new delightfully lyrical thought:

the same rhythmic figure thereupon builds up an independent gradation:

and finally, in a different position, gives the theme itself a new expression of impassioned desire:

The melodic flow of the whole of this first part prompted Dvořák's sensitive feeling for contrast to give the subordinate theme the expression of rhythmic animation and buoyant, overflowing good spirits:

2.

A very skilfully worked-out development draws first upon the basic elements of the principal theme. It then flares up passionately in a sharp skirmish between the principal and the subordinate theme, twisting and turning through numerous minor keys. After working up to a splendidly contrived climax, where another surprise awaits us: the recapitulation begins not only with the second thought of the principal theme (1*b*), but is in the unexpected key of G major! The recapitulation then runs its normal course, concluding, however, with a coda in which the final culmination of the movement is held up for a while by a quietly reminiscent dialogue between the two main thoughts comprising the principal theme (1*a* and 1*b*).

Second place in the cycle of movements in this Quartet is given to the Scherzo movement *(Molto vivace,* F minor with Trio in D flat major, ³/₄), which is undoubtedly Dvořák's loveliest Scherzo as well as one of the loveliest single movements in the whole of musical literature. It is in three-part form with completely parallel outer parts, the subject-matter of the whole movement evolving out of a single, *furiant*-like syncopated element. In addition, each of the three main parts of the movement divides up again into three paragraphs, in which partial symmetry is maintained only in the Trio. The outer parts of the Scherzo, which have the air of a very vivacious and light-footed dance are given their own theme which seems to trip gracefully in a delicate "skočná" rhythm on a higher plane (3*a*) before coming down firmly to earth with a much more solid stamping final clause:

3*a*.

In the second paragraph, the theme is combined with a counter-point of this final clause in sequence:

whereas the third paragraph makes use of this phrase alone, but gives it a melodic line:

In the Trio which, though much quieter in tone, is filled with an ineffably tender fervency, the first paragraph presents, in a calm dialogue between the first violin and the 'cello, a new broadly flowing theme built up from the basic rhythmic element and endowed with singular melodic beauty:

The second paragraph of the Trio transposes the theme to the dominant, while the third presents it in canonic imitation in the two violins, the expression rising to such heights of ecstasy as if a whole choir of larks were soaring and singing from full throats above a country bathed in golden sunlight. This glorious song dies away in the lingering notes of the first violin over a soft pedal point of the chord of D flat major, in which an echo of the closing bars of the aria "The smile of a child" from Dvořák's opera "The Jacobin"

is another proof of what feelings of bliss and felicity were the source of the emotional inspiration from which this work sprang.*

The same feelings permeate the content of the slow third move-ment *(Lento e molto cantabile,* F major, $^4/_4$) whose strongly romantic character is full of sweetly melodious and ardent yearning. This is immediately apparent in the calm, softly melting and melodically folk-coloured theme, each of its two periods (5*a* and 5*b*) being twice presented, each time in the first part of the movement in a four-part setting:

In the middle part, the minor tonality and the chromatic line of the theme above the pedal point of a rhythmic ostinato of triplets:

only slightly disturbs the tranquil current of the movement, without weakening the expression of that ineffable happiness of which Dvořák spoke in his letter and which permeates the whole Quartet. On the contrary, its rapture makes itself felt all the more strongly when, after a short central intermezzo, the lyrical *cantabile* of the

* The day before Christmas Eve, 1895, when in the middle of writing this movement, Dvořák wrote to his friend Alois Göbl at Sychrov by Turnov: "We are, praise be to God, all well and rejoice at being spared after three years to spend this dear and happy Christmas festival in Bohemia. How different did we feel last year in America, where we were so far away in a foreign country and separated from all our children and friends. But the Lord God has vouch-safed us this happy moment and that is why we feel so inexpressibly content!"

introductory part (5*a* and 5*b*) returns, this time as if with a charming smile playing on its lips in the form of a playful demisemiquaver figure of a contrapuntal second and the march-like rhythm of the pizzicato in the viola and violoncello. The section mounts to an amazingly beautiful climax whereupon, after a short allusion to the theme of the middle part, the rising melody in the violins brings the movement to a close in the home tonic of F major and in a mood of meditative bliss.

The fourth movement *(Allegro non tanto*, A flat major, ²/₄) is the organic culmination of the thought-content of the whole quartet, in mood youthfully gay throughout, while some of the themes have a Czech folk-music colouring. In form it is a combination of the sonata and rondo forms with three themes. The first—a lively polka-like tune—does not enter in its proper form (7*a*) till the 12th bar after being previously announced in a 'cello solo and by the violin in a variant (7*b*) which also has an important say later in the movement:

The theme is discussed at considerable length and there is even time to develop an episode based on its own derivative:

Only after a diversion created by a gay running semiquaver figure, quite typical of the movement (Ex. 8), does it make way for the calmer melody of the second theme:

8.

9.

But it is only a temporary tranquillization and concentration of expression, for it is not long before the rhythmic figure 8 disturbs the line and theme 7*b* introduces a mischievously unsettling element, this time in the following guise:

7*d.*

In the same way, the third theme of the movement, perhaps of all the themes the one most deeply tinged with the spirit of Czech folk-music:

10.

with its characteristic *molto cantabile* (in G flat major) and its deeply emotional quality, introduces into the movement a firm but smoothly flowing line of melody. Yet even its serious close can change in a flash to a jocular mood, especially when it is artfully provoked by the sportive variant of the principal theme (7*b*) skipping teasingly from one instrument to another. This variant is also made use of in a kind of short development in which the original as well as an augmented version of the thought perform all sorts of vagaries, with the agile semiquavers of 7*b* constantly on the run. Thereupon, in the form of a recapitulation, there are reviewed, with appropriate modulation changes, all the above-quoted themes as at the beginning of the movement. The composition then ends swith a fairly long coda based on motifs *7a*, *b* and *c*, the basic mood mounting to an expression of exuberant high spirits.

QUARTET IN G MAJOR
for two violins, viola and violoncello. — Opus 106.

First movement written in score between the 11th and the 19th, the second between the 21st and the 24th, the third completed on the 28th November, the fourth on the 9th December 1895.—First performed by the Bohemian Quartet (Hoffmann, Suk, Nedbal, Wihan) in Prague, on October 9th 1896.—Published in summer 1896 by Simrock.—Duration: 38 minutes.

Detailed reference has already been made in the introductory paragraphs to the analysis of the Quartet in A flat major (see p. 104) to the fact that the G major Quartet, op. 106, closely preceded the composition of the Quartet in A flat major, op. 105, as the first of Dvořák's compositions to be written after his definitive return home from abroad. The G major Quartet is also, in the main, a work of gay good humour and warm lyricism, its musical expression having also cast off the distinguishing features of the "American" period of Dvořák's creation, though not so completely as in the A flat major Quartet, for here and there, like a reminiscence, an exotically coloured idea comes through. In the high quality of the musical content and the compositional mastery with which it is written, the G major Quartet has also its place among the most outstanding manifestations of the composer's genius.

The first movement *(Allegro moderato*, G major, $^2/_4$) calls up quite unmistakably the basic mood of smiling content and inner happiness. The playful, fluttering principal theme with which the movement opens combines forthwith two thematic elements which are frequently employed independently in the structure of the movement:

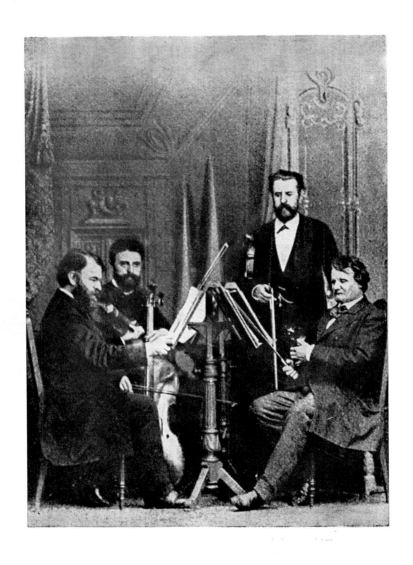

5. The Joachim Quartet, Berlin
(Josef Joachim, Robert Hausmann, Emanuel Wirth, Hegemeister)

6. Facsimile of the first page of the score of the String Quartet in A flat major

The same spring freshness as distinguishes the theme is apparent in the energetic transitional motif:

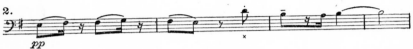

especially when, after its first entry in a minor key, in which the characteristic minor seventh reappears, it swings into a bright major mode and, partnered by the triplet figure of the principal theme (1*b*), breaks into a spirited dancing measure. An expressive and song-like element in the movement is the folk-coloured subordinate theme which continues for some time in the key of B flat major, but also partly in B major, its exposition taking the place of a closing theme:

Truly masterly is the development section of this movement. With unfailing resource the composer's creative fancy interweaves and alternates the two basic elements of the principal theme (1) with the clear-cut rhythms of the transitional theme (2), passing at the same time from the starting-point of B flat major, suggested at the close of the exposition in a complicated modulational process through the keys of F sharp major, E minor, B minor and G minor to A flat major, at which point there is the tenderest of allusions to the melodic subordinate theme (3) followed by a quick change to E major. A boldly built-up gradation based on motif 2 opens into a sudden tranquilization in G major, which also marks the beginning of the recapitulation. This is carried through with great compositional art and with the spontaneity of thought that is the true mark of genius. The same remarkable fertility of fancy distinguishes the recapitulation. This section contains an enrichment of the principal theme with a new countermelody of a lyrically melting character:

omitting, however, before the entry of the subordinate theme the broad episode based on theme 2 which, in a powerful and jubilant conclusion, sets the crown on the whole movement.

The second movement *(Adagio ma non troppo,* E flat major, $^3/_8$), the culminating part of the work, is one of the loveliest and most profound slow movements in Dvořák's creation. The author of the "Dumky" is clearly recognizable in its impassioned sensibility and ardent Slav lyricism, nor is a certain meditativeness typical of the movement able to affect the general mood of the Adagio, which mirrors, above all, the infinite peace and bliss of an inexpressibly happy soul. The form of the movement is determined by the free alternation of two paragraphs, one in a major and the other in a minor tonality, but with a common thematic base. The theme itself is full of manly depth of feeling borne on a broad stream of melody and breathing a profound sense of calm despite its melodic compass of more than two octaves, and despite the fact that, having opened with a grave melody on the sonorous G string of the violin (4*a*) it shows a considerable rise in melodic and emotional tension at its conclusion (4*b*). If at the beginning of the movement there are intimations of yearning in the variant in E flat minor (4*c*), it only provides the greater contrast to the ardour of its colouring in the tonic key of E flat major, a contrast further strengthened by the contrapuntal line of the second violin and of the viola:

The change into E flat minor, signalled by an ostinato figure in the violoncello accompaniment somewhat softens and veils the expression of the theme (4c) but does not diminish its emotional intensity, especially when the gradation based on its third bar, with its broad span of a descending seventh (4d), revives the expression of intense desire.

The middle part of the movement raises to still greater heights the beauty, richness and purity of the emotion of the two main paragraphs. The basic theme in E flat major is now delivered by the violin in a higher register above a rich figural accompaniment, whereupon, after a modulation through E flat minor, the key in which the movement opened, its minor variant (4c) appears passionately agitated in F sharp minor, concluding its massed gradation with a festive and powerful *grandioso* presentation of the basic theme in C major. Here the movement reaches its climax. As if an organ were to sound forth with all its stops out, the four instruments declaim the theme in an imposing harmony of chords spread over

three or four strings. After a general pause, a calm minor echo of
the "*grandioso*" directs the stream of the movement into the home
tonic in which the principal theme returns in its original shape. But
only in its first clause (4*a*), for the final clause (4*b*) blossoms into a
melodically and emotionally mighty coda, which runs its course
in the rapturous tones of pure Czech melody.

The third movement, the Scherzo, contains the clearest echoes,
in expression and mood, of Dvořák's sojourn across the seas and, on
listening to it, one cannot but call to mind the similar character of
the Scherzo movement in the "From the New World" Symphony
and in the String Quartet, op. 97. The form is again three-part, the
outer parts, however, not being identical, as the first section, itself
in ternary form, returns considerably abridged after the Trio. This
first part *(Molto vivace, B minor, ³/₄)*, in spite of the minor mode, is
in the nature of an extremely lively "skočná" embodied in the two
principal thematic ideas of which one hops nimbly along (5*a*) while
the other, taking over in part the rhythm of the first with which it
combines in canonic imitation, steps out in vigorous good spirits
(5*b*):

The middle part in A flat major, rhythmically quieter than the
first, is composed of a smoothly phrased pentatonic theme, presented in dialogue form by the viola and violin:

and, on the other, of a simple thought stepping out quietly in duple time:

The Trio part of the movement *(Un poco meno mosso,* D major, $^3/_4$) is, as compared with the basic rhythmic stir of the Scherzo, an intermezzo of smiling idyllic content. The theme begins in broken triads over a soft pedal of chords, with a wave-like rise and fall (7*a*), then makes a diatonic run into high trills, and ends in a phrase typically Dvořák in its "skočná" rhythm (7*b*):

In the course of several expositions of the theme, there are passages of intoxicating melodic beauty in which all the parts join, the first violin, however, assuming the lead and showing a particular fondness for soaring up into its highest registers. The third part of the movement is a recapitulation of the first, shortened, however, by the omission of the whole middle episode based on theme 6 in the major mode.

The fourth movement (Finale, G major) is, for Dvořák, remarkably free; indeed, the impression is almost one of improvisation, even though it is based on a rondo scheme. It begins with a slow six-bar introduction *(Andante sostenuto,* $^4/_4$) in which the principal theme, beginning with a furiant-like syncopation and ending with a similarly furiant-like stamp, proceeds without delay from a very quiet augmentation to its proper form:

8. **Allegro con fuoco**

This marks the beginning of the quick part of the movement *(Allegro con fuoco,* $^2/_4$), for the most part very lively in mood but also, in places, pensively overcast. The first of these nuances of mood is embodied both in the character of the principal theme, its small figures skipping light-heartedly over the quick-running demisemiquaver figurations, as well as in the emotionally tense second theme which, in its melodic line and in its rhythmic and harmonic ostinato (in G minor) is a kind of involuntary reminiscence of the primitive musical expression of American native peoples:

9.

The first return of theme 8 (in D flat major with a modulation to G major) effects a considerable tranquilization in which, while the lively basic movement shows no signs of flagging, there is a fairly long exposition of the more softly emotional third theme. This theme begins with a small, swelling figure, taken over by each of the instruments in turn:

10.

In its further development it appears in many different variants, now rhythmically more sharply profiled, now more lyrical and softly phrased. Theme 8 then re-enters, first in its original shape and later in a calm augmentation, *Andante sostenuto*, as in the introduction its expression of peaceful reconciliation preparing for the pensive mood of the intermezzo, of interest for the way in which it works exclusively with quotations from the first movement. The main say is given here to a variant of the subordinate theme (3) which, with a shift into the key of E minor and over the deep pedal point of a tonic fifth in the 'cello, is now tinged with a pensive melancholy even giving the impression, in the closing figure delivered in unison by the violin and viola (with an American seventh!), of a gravely fervent psalm-tune:

A three-stage shift into a major key (C, F and B major), in which both elements of the principal theme from the first movement (1*a* and *b*) are recalled, does not succeed in dispelling a certain wistfulness which is confined not only to the intermezzo, but interrupts no less than three times the new presentations of the themes of the last movement which are now reviewed in reverse order (10, climax based on motif 3*a*, 9 and 8). Not till the reminiscence of the softly affective theme 3 has passed through the keys of G, A flat and A major, does the composer seem to throw off the curious dreaminess which has so long held him under its spell: theme 10 rises in a steep gradation to theme 8, and this, in a spirit of renewed good humour and gaiety, concludes the movement and the quartet.

THE CYPRESSES

Twelve Compositions for String Quartet based on Poems by Gustav Pfleger-Moravský

Composed in the form of songs between July 11th and 27th, 1865, arranged for string quartet between April 21st and 27th and May 20th and 21st, 1887.—Nos. 1, 2, 3, 9 and 11 were performed under the title: "Evening Songs" by Karel Ondříček, Jan Pelikán, Petr Mareš and Alois Neruda at a concert of the "Umělecká Beseda" on January 6th, 1888 in Prague.—Nos. 1—9 and no. 11 (renumbered no. 10) were published under the title "The Cypresses", revised by Josef Suk and published under the title "The Cypresses" by "Hudební Matice Umělecké Besedy", Prague, in 1921.—Duration of the individual pieces: 2—4 minutes.

A quite exceptional place in Dvořák's compositions for two violins, viola and violoncello, and, indeed, in the whole body of the composer's chamber music, is held by these twelve small compositions, being an arrangement by the Master for this group of instruments of songs which he wrote at the very beginning of his creative career as his first vocal compositions. It was in the year 1865, when still a viola-player in the Czech Interim Theatre Orchestra, that he composed eighteen songs to texts from the collection of poems entitled "The Cypresses" by Gustav Pfleger-Moravský, which title he also gave to his songs. Though the cycle includes a number of songs written as an expression of love and pride for his country, they are, for the most part, the intimate confession of unrequited love for the charming young actress of the Czech Interim Theatre, Josefina Čermáková. For the woman who later became his sister-in-law (Dvořák married her younger sister Anna) and the wife of Count Václav Kaunic, Dvořák cherished life-long feelings of sincere admiration and affection and so the songs, "The Cypresses", which had been inspired by this first passion, were particularly dear to him. Though the songs were not published in their original form during the composer's lifetime, he returned to them again and again with curious persistency in order to make use of the music in other ways.

This he did most effectively in the 'eighties, not only rewriting twelve of them in masterly fashion (four as op. 2 in 1880, and eight as "Love Songs", op. 83, in 1888) but, in addition, making an arrangement of these last eight and four others, in the spring of 1887, for two violins, viola and violoncello without any vocal part.

Thus the quartet arrangement of "The Cypresses" is, perhaps, the most interesting proof of how strong was the tie which bound Dvořák to his first collection of songs. For if he found it necessary in revising these compositions as songs to make certain changes— especially for the sake of good declamation—even in their musical structure, in rewriting them for string quartet he kept them altogether unchanged, both as regards the melodic line and the rhythm and harmony, the only alteration being a shift of key in no. 11 from A flat major. The transcription was thus actually confined to the instrumentation of the different parts and then, in several cases, where the songs were unusually short, to lengthening them either by simple repetition (5, 11) or by repetition with an interchange of parts (1, 2, 4 and 9). But even in the instrumentation of these quartet compositions, Dvořák kept to the original simple character of the songs, assigning the melody of the vocal part to a single instrument while the other three provide the accompaniment.

It is unnecessary to analyse the thematic structure of these miniature pieces or illustrate it with examples. They are simple songforms, calmly vocal in character, based on a single main thematic idea, their form developing naturally from the line and mood of the words to which they are set and not in accordance with any purely musical principles of construction. They are, however, undoubtedly pieces of true Dvořák charm and individuality which, especially in the atmosphere of intimate "Hausmusik", provide a welcome addition to the repertoire, with which recommendation he offered them very soon after their completion—though unsuccessfully at that time—to his publisher Simrock.

B. QUARTETS FOR STRINGS AND PIANO OR HARMONIUM

QUARTET IN D MAJOR
for violin, viola, violoncello and piano.—Opus 23.

Written in score between May 24th and June 10th, 1875.—First performed by Václav Kopta, Petr Mareš, Alois Neruda and Karel ze Slavkovských at a concert of the musical section of the "Umělecká beseda" on December 16th, 1880, in Prague.—Published by Schlesinger, Berlin, in 1880.—Duration: 33 minutes.

The first of the two piano quartets is the last of the trilogy of intimate compositions which Dvořák wrote in quick succession in the spring of 1875 as a preamble to the great creative gesture of the following F major Symphony and the opera "Vanda". In the short period of a few weeks, it was preceded by the Piano Trio in B flat major, op. 21, and the Serenade in E major for String Orchestra, op. 22, both works showing a rapidly maturing creative personality and unusual skill in the handling of the musical material. The Piano Quartet in D major may not, perhaps, take first place in this trilogy as regards the melodic flowering of the thoughts, for it is the most intimate of them both in expression and mood, but certainly it rises above them in the very individual conception of form. Here Dvořák gives a particularly interesting and convincing proof of the reach and daring of his compositional imagination. This is true not only of the formal arrangement of the whole work, in respect of which the quartet is among Dvořák's few compositions comprising only three movements, the function of the Scherzo movement being combined with that of the finale, but also the internal design of the three movements is here, though perfectly logical, to a great extent free and original.

The first movement (*Allegro moderato*, D major, $^3/_4$), emotionally changeable, is interesting especially for its varied thematic structure and no less varied modulations. The calm lyrical principal theme, with which the sonata movement opens over the measured quaver accompaniment in the piano, develops in the fundamental key out of a two-bar motif into an eight-bar period:

In the next eight bars, the theme is repeated in B major, the line of the last two bars now appearing in melodic inversion and providing the modulation from F sharp minor to the key of D major in which a new transitional theme sets out with great energy and bustle, and concludes with a fragment of the principal theme:

After presenting the theme in a wide range of keys, the stream of the movement opens into the dominant key of A major, in which the subordinate theme makes its entry:

This theme, softly pleasing in its melodic line, is repeated several times, alternately in the keys of A and E major and always in a different instrumentation and figuration, whereupon there follows the strongly rhythmic closing section based successively on three motifs, of which the first two have the same core (4a and b), while the third (5) is a derivation of the transitional theme 2.

Motif 5, which brings the exposition to a close, is given considerable importance in the development, which again shows a wide range of key. Grafted on to the recapitulation is a coda in which the subordinate theme 3 first combines in a highly effective *grandioso* with the principal theme (1), then, alone, sings wistfully in the 'cello. After a gradation based on the principal theme, it concludes the movement with a new *grandioso* of the three string instruments in unison, finally dying away in a quietly struck chord.

The second movement *(Andantino,* B minor, ²/₄) is written in the form of five variations and a coda on an original song theme in two periods. This pensively melancholy theme begins with an eight-bar period in B minor (regularly repeated), shifting in the middle eight bars into D major, while the last eight bars return to the tonic, most variations ending in a characteristic disconsolate Doric close through A major. This is how it begins:

Andantino cantabile

The variations, except for the fourth, which diverges into E flat major, maintain the tonal character of the theme but subject it to considerable melodic and rhythmic changes. The first variation is rhythmically clean-cut with characteristic syncopation, the second is more ornamentally expanded, the third has a vigorous, straightforward rhythm, the fourth embraces a broad melodic compass and the fifth breaks up the canonically imitated diatonic descent into small, irregular rhythmic figures:

The variations, though contrasted in movement and pace, are all permeated by an expression of pensive yearning and lively sensibility. A coda follows based on a variant close to the original theme and raising the movement to a climax of great melodic beauty and warmth of expression.

The third movement of the quartet is, as remarked above, one of those finales which in Dvořák's compositions combine the function of a Scherzo and a final movement, here clearly differen-

tiated and marked off from each other. The first is represented by a
Scherzo *(Allegretto scherzando,* D major, $^3/_8$), with the flowing waltz-
like movement that distinguishes the theme, tinged at first with a
slight melancholy which, however, encouraged by the lively motif 8,
it then throws off completely:

The second section *(Allegro agitato,* $^4/_4$), a shade more flexible and
happy in mood, develops more or less in the form of variations on
this theme:

9.   Allegretto agitato

The first time the theme is set in the dominant key of A major, but
in the course of its development, enriched with counterpoints, it
passes through a number of keys. The return to the Scherzo section
is a strict repetition of the first, to which is added a kind of development, livelier and then quieter in character. The second section
brings the movement back to the home tonic of D major and, after
a somewhat irregular development of its theme (9), concludes with
a quick-paced variation of the same theme in $^6/_8$ time. A sudden
falling-off in tone at the very end only confirms the generally restrained mood of the composition.

BAGATELLES

for two violins, violoncello and harmonium. — Opus 47.

The score of the first movement was written on May 1st, the second between the 8th and 9th, the third and fourth on the 9th and the fifth on the 12th of the same month, 1878.—First performed at a musical matinée of the Umělecká beseda on February 2nd, 1879. The players were: Ferdinand Lachner, Vorel, Alois Neruda and the composer.—Published by Simrock, Berlin, in a four-handed arrangement by Dr. Josef Zubatý, in 1879, and in 1880, in the original form, under the title "Bagatelles" and with the composer's dedication "To My Friend Josef Srb-Debrnov". (The harmonium may be replaced by the piano).— Duration: 22 minutes.

Dvořák was at work on the first series of "Slavonic Dances" when he received a request from a group of chamber music enthusiasts, with whom he himself played either viola or harmonium, to write something for the above unusual combination of strings and harmonium. It took him only a few days to fulfil the request, and thus it was that the Quartet "Bagatelles" came to be written.

His intention was to write nothing more than "Trifles", and so he contented himself with small movements in ternary rondo form based on, at most, two themes and with no hint of sonata form. This circumstance, however, did not deter him from showing his creative genius even within the limits of intimate little works for private performance, and not only in the charm of the separate musical thoughts growing out of the individuality of the different instruments, but also in the virtuosity with which he handles the material and in the beauty and fine gradations of his tone-colour. Nor did he fail to do justice to his sensitive feeling for formal neatness of design in the working out of the individual parts.

The first movement *(Allegretto scherzando,* G minor, $^2/_4$) grows out of a theme for which the composer, with a clear grasp of the characteristic instrumental colouring, made witty use of the middle part of the Czech folk-song "The Bagpipes Were Playing":

In the middle of the movement, this jolly little tune combines with a countermelody of a more smoothly-phrased and melting character:

The second movement, which follows the first without transition, is designated a minuet (Tempo di Minuetto, *Grazioso*, G major, $^3/_4$), but both in the systematically dotted rhythm of the main theme (2) as well as in its smoothly-phrased variant in the middle of the movement (2*a*), it approaches more closely in type to the Czech "sousedská".

The third movement *(Allegretto scherzando*, G minor, $^2/_4$) returns to the theme of the first movement (1), but adds two new variations, of which the first is enlivened by a hopping figuration in the violins (3a), while the second, strongly accented, is in polka rhythm (3b):

The whole exposition of these thoughts, the last being the most broadly presented, is repeated, the only divergence being that the third polka-like motif forming a kind of coda, assumes considerable refinement of expression and, at the end of the movement, floats gently away into the distance.

The fourth movement *(Andante con moto*, E major, $^3/_8$), which stands in place of the slow movement, is written in canon throughout on this calm, softly flowing and melodically very charming theme:

The canon is mainly two in one, with an interval of one bar, whether its line is divided between violin and violoncello or violin and harmonium, and only in the middle of the movement, in a short episode in G sharp major, does it change to three in one, the strings entering one after another at quaver intervals. In spite of the comparative simplicity of the compositional structure, it is a movement of great lyrical beauty and emotional depth.

The fifth movement *(Poco allegro*, G major, $^2/_4$) closes the

whole cycle in the style of a gay, spirited polka embodied in the
lively rhythm of the principal theme:

Otherwise the expression of this movement is related to that of the
first and third movements and gives to the whole work the impression of unity by again using a variant of theme 1 as the theme of its
middle part:

In the spontaneity of their musical invention, the "Bagatelles"
have much in common with the "Slavonic Dances", which are very
close to them in time and with which they also share a generally
humorous conception, though—being much more intimate in style
—they do not approach their riotous high spirits.

QUARTET IN E FLAT MAJOR
for violin, viola, violoncello and piano. — Opus 87.

Written in sketch between the 10th and 12th of August, and in score between
the 12th and 19th of the same month, 1889.—First performed in Prague at a
concert of the Umělecká beseda, held on November 23rd, 1890, the performers
being: Ferdinand Lachner, Petr Mareš, Hanuš Wihan and Hanuš Trneček.—
Published by Simrock early in 1890.—Duration: 34 minutes.

The second piano quartet, which was Dvořák's answer to the
request expressed a number of times by his publisher Simrock,
dates not only from the same period but is, if we limit our view to
his cyclic compositions in absolute music, also related in mood and

expression to the Piano Quintet in A major, op. 81, and the G major Symphony, op. 88. It is the period of Dvořák's full maturity, both as a man and as an artist, following upon a phase of development marked by a partial return to classicism, a time of strong inner clarification and broad range of mood; in short, the period of the creation of the opera "The Jacobin". As in the music of the symphony in G major, which closely preceded it, so in the music of the E flat major Quartet, one recognises an artist gifted with a rich and expressively original fund of musical invention, unafraid of making substantial departures from traditional norms and, at the same time, possessed of a wide emotional and spiritual compass, capable of expressing himself with grave decision and frankness, yet always with rare sensibility. In the rich flowering of the composer's thoughts, in the masterly craft with which he handles his themes, and in the beauty of its harmony, this quartet is worthy to take its place by the side of the quintet, than which it is, indeed, more balanced in mood and much more concentrated and coherent in design.

The mood of the first movement *(Allegro con fuoco*, E flat major, $^4/_4$) is determined forthwith by the character of the principal theme, which strongly predominates in the thematic structure, while the secondary theme is limited to its presentation in the exposition and recapitulation. The principal theme comprises a first strain which, in a unison statement in the strings covering a compass of three octaves, sets out with firm and resolute step. The second strain is rhythmically more agitated and varied, but no less lively and virile, whether the piano joins in with a descending (1*b*) or an ascending passage (1*c*):

After a short discussion in which the rhythmic elements are successively diminished, the first strain of the theme (1*a*) is repeated in a buoyantly soaring mood with nimble figurations in the piano, followed by a transitional thought whose light carefree rhythms are derived from motif 1*c*:

this, in a modulation through B minor to G major, prepares for the entry of the subordinate theme, contrasting with its predecessors in its softly melodic and yet emotionally impassioned line:

The theme is first delivered by the viola, then by the violin and finally, in a new presentation with rich figural embroidery, by the piano to which is assigned the re-entry of the principal theme (1*a*) in the function of a closing theme with whose exposition the section ends.

The lively development works exclusively with 1*a* and 1*c*, while the recapitulation, omittimg the episodic motifs 1*c* and 2, starts away with the subordinate theme (3), which begins tenderly in B major disturbed by the plaintive interval of G—F sharp in the violoncello (an inspired stroke) and only then making a quick jump to the key of E flat major in which it sings with full-throated ardour. The movement closes with a boldly modulating coda, the powerful impression of which is plastically underlined by a sudden decline to a very delicate intermezzo just before the close.

The second movement *(Lento,* G flat major, ⁴/₄) is not only among the loveliest slow movements in thought-content and the most deeply moving in mood which Dvořák created, but also holds a special place because of its unusual formal design. It comprises two thematically and structurally identical parts, based on five themes and a short final phrase, which may be looked upon either as a thematically doubled binary form or a kind of exposition and recapitulation in sonata form in which the development is omitted. The introductory paragraph in the first part of the movement is permeated in content and rhythmic and harmonic disposition with the expression of deep, undisturbed peace. It opens with a grave theme of manly strength of feeling which is twice repeated, each time with an increase in volume as well as in richness of harmonic colouring:

The second theme, which follows immediately on the first, is still calmer in expression. Simply, without any dynamic rise and fall and in very delicate tone-colouring, it is sung by the violin, to a gently undulating accompaniment divided alternately between the viola and piano:

It then closes into the third theme, rhythmically and dynamically somewhat more lively and also more agitated in feeling:

out of which there suddenly develops a resolute transition to the next paragraph which, in sharp contrast to the tranquility of the preceding one, introduces an expression of strongly passionate tension:

The agitated mood is not, however, of long duration, for another new theme, the fifth and last, somewhat reminiscent of theme 6, and again breathing an expression of celestial calm and purity of feeling, concludes the first part of the movement very delicately and dreamily:

The whole of the first Lento part is now repeated in its original form as regards content and structure, but with a few unimportant digressions in the instrumentation and tonalities. The calm statement of theme 8 concludes the movement in the pure and luminous tone-colouring of higher spheres.

The third movement, the Scherzo, is in regular ternary form, the completely indentical outer parts (*Allegro moderato, grazioso*, E flat major, $^3/_4$) themselves being also in three parts. The movement and mood of these parts, in which a mildly sportive tone alternates with a light melancholy, have close affinities with the Scherzo movement of the neighbouring G major Symphony. The first of its two themes is in quiet dancing measure, not without an air of refined elegance:

Allegro moderato, grazioso

The second, in its melodic line and characteristic augmented second (E flat—F sharp) and in the monotonous effect of a pedal point on the chord of G minor, has something of an oriental colouring:

The middle Trio section *(Un pochettino piu mosso*, B major) shows a considerable heightening of mood due to the lively sinuous triplets in the accompaniment as well as to the principal theme itself, whose hopping rhythm cannot but call to mind the transitional motif 2 in the first movement:

Un pochettino piu mosso

The whole Scherzo, delicately balanced and rounded off is full of the magic of exquisite melodic and harmonic refinement.

The fourth movement *(Allegro ma non troppo*, E flat major, $^2/_2$) is similar in character and structure to the first movement. It is emotionally more explosive and also more condensed in form. A striking feature is the unusually free harmonic and modulating plan; the movement is actually written in E flat minor and reaches the tonic of E flat major only after the recapitulation and with the entry of the transitional theme. The principal theme is equally energetic and rhythmically expressive, though livelier in pace than the principal theme of the first movement, and in the same way, too, opens the movement in unison octaves enriched, on a second repetition, with figurations and harmonic colouring:

The exposition of the theme is followed by a bustling transitional paragraph in the key of G flat major, of which the two thoughts—one vigorous and lively, the other, in canonic imitation, tinged with yearning—are derived from the principal theme:

An enharmonic modulation from G flat major to F sharp major prepares for the entry of the secondary theme in B major which, like the secondary theme in the first movement, introduces a contrasting element of rare melodic beauty and warmth of feeling:

A delicate closing theme concludes the exposition in the key of F sharp major:

Once again the last movement provides a parallel with the first. The middle part (the development) is based on the principal theme alone (including its variant 12*a*), and it continues in the same wide excursions into divergent keys as the exposition. These unusually varied and unorthodox modulations come to an end with the recapitulation in the tonic key of E flat, in which the individual themes are reviewed and built up to a jubilant and dynamically brilliant conclusion.

IV

COMPOSITIONS FOR THREE INSTRUMENTS

A. TRIOS FOR STRING INSTRUMENTS

TERCETTO IN C MAJOR
for two violins and viola.—Opus 74.

Written in score between January 7th and 14th, 1887.—First performed by Karel Ondříček, JUDr. Jan Buchal and MUDr. Jaroslav Šťastný at a chamber music concert of the Umělecká beseda, on March 30th, 1887, in Prague.— Published by Simrock, Berlin, in May 1887.—Duration: 22 minutes.

The unusual combination of two violins and a viola was the ensemble for which Dvořák wrote two compositions within a month, and in close succession, in answer to the same request as had formerly led to the writting of "Bagatelles", op. 48. Both were intended for performance by a little group of enthusiastic amateurs, one of the violinists being a beginner and the other—Dvořák himself. Both were, for that reason, very simple and intimate compositions, the first of which having proved technically rather more difficult than was intended was published by the composer in its original form. This was the Tercetto in C major, op. 74, which alone forms a cyclic whole closely conforming to the types established in chamber music. Thus arose a work which, in the charm of its themes and of their handling, as well as in the beauty of its instrumentation, shows the hand of Dvořák all the more clearly, the simpler the form and the more modest the demands made on the executant.

The first movement *(Introduzione, Allegro ma non troppo*, C major, ⁴/₄) is a small three-part form in which the quietly lyrical outer parts:

1. Allegro ma non troppo

mp espress. ———— ≤ *f*

are contrasted with a rhythmically more energetic idea, constantly enlivened by a semiquaver figuration:

2.

mp   *cresc.*   *f*

The whole movement seems to be designed as an introduction to the slow second movement into which a number of modulating chords lead from the abruptly concluded third part.

The second movement *(Larghetto,* F major, ⁶/₈) blooms into a delicate and warmly emotional song, similar in form to the first and with similarly contrasted themes. Of these the one moving gently over a quaver accompaniment is romantically coloured:

3. Larghetto
      dolce

mf molto espress. ≤ *f*   *dim.*   *p*

while the other, in canonic imitation, disturbs the quiet tenor of the movement with its livelier rhythmic character:

4.

The movement then closes with an expression of dreamy and sensitive beauty.

The third movement *(Scherzo, Vivace,* A minor, ³/₄) altogether preserves the formal character of the clasical Scherzo with parallel outer parts separated by a calmer Trio *(Poco meno mosso,* A major).

Its whole character openly acknowledges its author's spiritual affinity with Schubert. The expression of the outer parts is very lively and rhythmically restless, as is the theme out of which it grows:

5. Vivace

The middle part, on the other hand, has a warmly coloured theme with a melodically attractive and more supple line:

6. Poco meno mosso

whose inherent charm is shown to even greater advantage in the course of the exposition and the characteristic modulational transitions.

The fourth movement (*Thema con Variazioni*, Poco adagio, C major, $^2/_4$) concludes the work with a small set of variations on an original theme in the archaistic tone of a dramatically grave recitative:

7. Poco adagio

The variations, of which there are ten in all, are very short and are based for the most part on the series of basic harmonies indicated in the example. Their arrangement and treatment in alternating quick and slow tempos is as charming in its changing moods as the fertility of resource shown in the rhythmic and contrapuntal detail is inexhaustible, so that it provides a truly masterly conclusion to the whole work.

TERCETTO "BAGATELLES"
(ROMANTIC PIECES)
for two violins and viola. — (Opus 75 a)

Written about January 20th, 1887.—First performed by Willibald Schwejda, Herbert Berger and Ladislav Černý at a concert of the Prague Quartet held on February 24th, 1938, in Prague.—Parts published by Hudební matice, Prague, in 1948.—Duration: 14 minutes.

In writing the second of the pair of tercettos, of which mention was made in the introduction to the analysis of the first above, Dvořák was careful to take into consideration the small technical accomplishment of the players, a factor to which were subordinated both the formal aspect and the content of the composition which he created with the same love and care as he devoted to any more ambitious work. "I'm now writing 'Bagatelles', just imagine—only for two violins and viola", he confided to his publisher Simrock while writing this tercetto (January 18th, 1887). "The work gives me as great pleasure as if I were writing a big symphony—but what do you think of it? They are certainly meant more for dilettantes, but did not Beethoven and Schumann write more than once with very modest means, and how!..." (Proof that Dvořák was fully satisfied with the music of this little work is the fact that, not wishing to publish two tercettos at once for the same unusual combination of instruments, he immediately arranged the second for publication under the tittle of "Romantic Pieces" for violin and piano, to which reference will be made at the end of this analysis.)

The manuscript score of the second tercetto has no title. Dvořák himself, in his letter to Simrock cited above, called the compositions "Bagatelles". It not being his intention to write an organically unified cycle, he simply grouped together four little compositions—mostly three-part—which, on transcribing them for violin and piano, he named according to their different moods: "Cavatina", "Capriccio", "Romance" and "Elegy" (Ballad), which titles, however, Dvořák omitted on publication. Each of these four parts grows out of a single theme and is in song form, all together making up a little work full of charming musical thoughts and delightful in tone-colouring. Dvořák's allusion in this connection to pieces of a similar character by Schumann is perfectly justifiable.

The first part (orig. Cavatina, *Moderato*, B flat major, $^4/_4$) opens with a calm, delicately pensive melody in the first violin (1)—swelling more passionately only in the middle paragraph (1*a*)—drawn over the sustained bass notes of the viola and the rhythmic *ostinato* accompaniment of the second violin:

The second part (orig. Capriccio, *Poco allegro*, D minor, $^2/_4$) is in the form of gay, carefree little variations on a simple, harmonically attractive folk-coloured theme which enters with resolute step, but quickly moderates its expression.

This piece, in which the theme undergoes no great transformations, is effective for its whimsicality of mood and expressive instrumentation.

The third part (orig. Romance, *Allegro*, B flat major, $^4/_4$), and the one most strongly reminiscent of Schumann, is sweetly dreamy in mood and very close to the first in form. It differs mainly in the greater warmth of expression and in the way the harmonically and melodically similar line has the support of a middle part in the second violin in the shape of quietly modulating triplets:

The fourth part of the tercetto (orig. Elegy and also Ballad, *Larghetto*, C minor, $^9/_8$) is relatively the most complex and also the most attractive of the group as regards both the thought and emotional content. It is a true elegy, strong and unaffected in its purity of feeling and poetry of mood. A short thematic fragment develops into a broad, grief-tinged flow of melody in the first violin above the long sustained chords of the other two instruments:

As already stated, Dvořák rewrote these four tercetto movements for violin and piano almost immediately after their composition (manuscript finished on January 25th, 1887), and had them published as "Romantic Pieces", op. 75. in May 1887, by Simrock. In transcribing the work he proceeded as follows: He left the musical content of the individual movements practically untouched, only making a slight alteration in the first one of the harmonic base in bars 30—36 (originally identical with bars 10—16) and, in the third movement, added three bars at the end. In addition, he gave the second of the group the new tempo indication—*Allegro maestoso* and changed that of the third to *Allegro appassionato*. The instrumental transcription was carried out so that in the "Romantic Pieces" the part of the first violin remained in the violin part and the supporting parts of the second violin and viola were given to the right hand and the left of the piano respectively. The only important change in stylisation is in the fourth movement, in which the sustained chords of the accompaniment are broken up into a serial semiquaver figuration. In this arrangement, suggested it is said by the musical critic, V. J. Novotný, a composition of Dvořák charm and refinement entered on a new career. ("Romantic Pieces" were first performed by Karel Ondříček and the composer at an evening of chamber music held on March 30th, 1887, in Prague. They were published by Simrock in the same year.)

B. TRIOS FOR STRINGS AND PIANO

TRIO IN B FLAT MAJOR
for violin, violoncello and piano.—Opus 21.

Score finished on May 14th, 1875 and partially revised in 1880.—First performed by František Ondříček, Alois Sládek and Karel ze Sladkovských at a concert held on February 17th, 1877.—Published by Schlesinger, Berlin, 1880. —Duration: 30 minutes.

The Trio in B flat major opens the series of Dvořák's piano trios with a youthfully sweeping and flexible gesture in the expressiveness and emotional purity of the musical matter and in the organisation and mastery of its forms. The work is the manifestation of a spon-

7. The Bohemian Quartet
(Karel Hoffmann, Hanuš Wihan, Oskar Nedbal, Josef Suk)

8. The Kneisel Quartet, Boston
(Frank Kneisel, Otto Roth, Louis Svecenski, Alwin Schroeder)

taneous upsurge of musical ideas which, separated by only a short space of time from the preceding quintet with double-bass, marked a further advance along the path to creative individuality, and provided as well a worthy predecessor to the Serenade for Strings which followed very soon afterwards. The whole work shows clearly that the musical content was the expression of a striving after something beautiful and noble, something to be fought for with joyful courage, while the tones of manly supplication and prayer issue from the lips.

The first movement *(Allegro molto*, B flat major, ²/₂) straightway establishes this content and mood, both in the character of the themes and in the spontaneous ease and creative élan with which the whole movement is conceived and realized. Melodically and in their inner expression all the themes are full of a concentrated nervous energy, and while providing the necessary contrast are also, to a considerable extent, inter-related, so that they follow and grow out of one another logically and without any forced transitions. Thus the principal theme (1), after a triple exposition in the keys of B flat major, G minor and E flat major successively, appears in the form of a sprightly diminution (1*a*), anticipating at the same time in its opening element (bracketed in Ex. 1*a*) a rocking ostinato over which is spread the calmer line of the transitional theme (2).

When this transitional theme yields to a new, more energetic and very proud variant of the principal theme (1*b*), its rhythmically firm steps are developed into the sharply syncopated rhythm and melodic rise and fall which constitute the characteristic features of the subordinate theme heard a few bars later. This is in the prescribed dominant of F major, and in the clear bell-like tones of the piano seems at first almost playful:

3 a.

In the course of its variational exposition in all three instruments, however, its true core is revealed as being also that of the closing theme created out of a melodic variant of its predecessor:

3 b.

The tension achieved by this theme suddenly collapses, but only to prepare the way for a new accumulation of tension in the development, where an elaborate modulational process of great variety is worked out at considerable length, exclusively employing the principal theme (1 and partly also 1*a*). The rising line continues into the recapitulation and the soaring coda. This last upsurge subsides after a few bars, as if conscious that the goal has not yet been reached, and theme 3*a* brings the movement to a gentle close.

The second movement *(Adagio molto e mesto,* G minor, ⁴/₈), after this sudden failing of strength, is like a fervently sincere petition for spiritual succour and support. The theme with which it opens is grave, calm, intensely ardent and even sombre in expression:

It is presented first by the solo piano, then by the violoncello followed by the violin, the voice of supplication sounding in its high registers with a special fervency of appeal. What was left unsaid is now delivered with equal eloquence by the second theme in the key of A major, which strikes a note of deeply passionate longing:

The two themes alternate in the course of the middle p..rt with increasing expressive force, until the second of them (5) gives full vent to its anguished yearning, while the first theme, (4) having made the return to G minor, sounds forth in the full sonority of a four-part canon. This, however, is the last upsurge of passion. Calm and confidence return to the soul, as is shown by the clear G major in which the delicate, serene augmentation of the first theme brings the movement to a close.

The third movement *(Allegretto scherzando,* E flat major, ²/₄) is, after this agitated prayer, a tranquilizing episode giving the opportunity for the gathering of new strength for the final victorious

contest in the last movement. The identical outer parts grow out
of a smilingly composed theme in polka measure:

The Trio, charming and refined in its musical thoughts, is in the
key of B major and, while continuing in duple time, is rhythmically
quieter and somewhat graver in mood. It is founded upon a theme
which unfolds in regular crotchet progression (7), combined at times
with an independent countermelody, and giving place in the middle
of the section to its more emotionally developed variant (7a):

The fourth movement (*Allegro vivace*, B flat major, $^6/_8$) sets
out straight away with a resolute readiness to do battle in a mood of
which there were intimations in the first movement. The expression
of all the themes is full of fighting spirit and confidence in the victorious outcome of the contest. The first opens the movement not, as
might be expected, in the tonic key of B flat major, but in a dark
G minor with a passionately agitated melodic line; the second advances in a vigorously proud marching rhythm (9) which is taken
over by the third, its chromatic line tense with suppressed feeling
(10) later hardening into a clarion call of great pomp. (10a).

At first the relatively short development works up all the elements of the subordinate theme (10, 10*a*), but then, quite unexpectedly, quotes the first theme from the slow movement (4) which, at a quicker pace and in lighter tones, sounds like the distant echo of difficulties overcome, and vanishes as suddenly as it appeared. The recapitulation shows some divergences from the exposition in the broader treatment of the first and second theme (8 and 9) and also in the entry of the third theme in G minor before it shifts to B flat major, and finally in the use of the first theme as it rises to a victoriously jubilant conclusion.

TRIO IN G MINOR
for violin, violoncello and piano. — Opus 26.

The first movement written in score between the 4th and the 9th, the second by the 12th, the third by the 14th and the fourth by the 20th of January, 1876. —First performed, as far as is known, by Ferdinand Lachner, Alois Neruda and the composer at a concert of Dvořák's works by the Choral Society in Turnov on June 29th, 1879.—Published by Bote & Bock, Berlin, in 1879. — Duration: $26^{1}/_{2}$ minutes.

The Piano Trio in G minor is separated from the preceding B flat major Trio by a period of only eight months. It is not surprising, therefore, that there should be no striking difference between the two compositions as regards development. In two respects, however, the trios differ very considerably. On the one hand, in their inner content, for the G minor—like the following String Quartet in E major—anticipates quite unmistakably the spiritual atmosphere of the Stabat Mater and, in contrast to the robustly optimistic and passionate yearning of the B flat major Trio, is predominantly expressive of spiritual anguish. And then, perhaps, not unconnected with this change in content, is the difference in structural design which, in the second of the trios, is distinguished by a frugality of thematic material such as is rare in Dvořák. No movement has more that two themes (the slow movement, indeed, only one) and what is more, the two themes are often closely related, thus strengthening the impression of thematic simplicity.

In the first movement *(Allegro moderato*, G minor, $^3/_4$), the principal theme is presented in two independent variants. The first is simpler and rhythmically more terse (1*a*), the second softer in expression and more decorative, with a characteristic syncopation in the second bar (1*b*):

1 *a.*   Allegro moderato

1 *b.*

Both variants alternate, while a delightful gradation with colourful modulations is built up on the second bar of the first variant. The subordinate theme grows out of a small motif which, repeated several times above a changing accompaniment, gives the impression of uneasy, unsatisfied desire:

The two basic themes (1a and 2) again alternate as the exposition runs its course, increasing the intensity of their unhappily agitated expression.

The same atmosphere prevails in the development, working in turn with all three thematic ideas and their constituent elements, and the same emotional tension is maintained in the recapitulation which introduces a number of changes in the order and treatment of the individual themes.

The second movement *(Largo,* E flat major, $^2/_4$) is built up on a single melodically and emotionally tense theme:

there is here a certain tendency towards formal three-part rondo form deriving from a kind of short development of elements of the theme in colourful modulations, in the middle of the movement. It is a Largo of characteristically Dvořák beauty and purity of emotional force, in which the calmer element in the spiritual mood of the composition achieves its highest plasticity of expression.

Nor does the third movement (Scherzo, *Presto,* G minor, $^3/_4$) diverge substantially from this basic mood. It is undoubtedly very lively and rhythmically well profiled, but these qualities are offset to a considerable extent by the minor key and also by the character of the themes. How little true gaiety, in spite of the crisp rhythms, is in the ten-bar theme presented at times in canonic imitation in the symmetrical outer parts (4) is clearly manifest in its sudden augmentation in the solo 'cello (4a), which holds up the rapid pace of the theme as if with a pensively unhappy reminiscence:

The Trio of the movement, in its clear G major and quiet thematic line, would seem to drop balsam into a spirit torn and bleeding,
soothing in its action rather than raising it to a mood of gaiety and
joy:

The composition first shakes itself free of this mood of painful
sensibility in the fourth movement *(Allegro non tanto,* G minor,
$^2/_4$) based again on two themes. The first falls into two distinct
strains: a thought setting out with great decision and then losing
confidence (6), and the shy hesitancy of a polka-motif broken up
into a little figure (7):

Both elements alternate several times, the first appearing finally in
a frolicking variant that has freed itself from all its former uncertainty:

The short subordinate theme, which enters first in the 'cello, is itself quite composed, but considerably enlivened by a counterpoint derived from motif 7:

The inner liveliness of the movement comes out more and more clearly in the gay rhythms of the development and the recapitulation which, opening with the entry of the subordinate theme 8, at last reaches the bright key of G major in which the composition ends in a mood of jollity and good humour.

TRIO IN F MINOR
for violin, violoncello and piano. — Opus 65.

First movement written in score between the 4th and 19th of February, the second (later shifted to third place) by the 6th of March, the third (finally the second) between the 7th and the 19th and the fourth between the 20th and the 31st of March, 1883.— First performed by Ferdinand Lachner, Alois Neruda and the composer at a concert of Dvořák's works given by the Boleslav Choral Society in Mladá Boleslav, on October 27th, 1883.—Published by Simrock, Berlin, 1883.—Duration: 39$^{1}/_{2}$ minutes.

The Piano Trio in F minor holds a similarly exceptional place in Dvořák's chamber music to that of his D minor Symphony in the sphere of symphonic music. Written a year earlier, it grows out of the same spiritual climate. Instead of smiling, untroubled cheerfulness, unaffected warmth and a spontaneous joy in living, otherwise so typical of Dvořák's disposition, the music of the Trio in F minor is the expression of a deeply-felt and passionate revolt and of disturbing questions to which he is still seeking the answer. Not even the Scherzo a la Capriccioso, with its stubbornly persistent rhythms, is able to throw off this basic mood, while the splendid Adagio, one of the loveliest among the many jewels of Dvořák's creation, has a principal theme full of spiritual suffering and a middle part full of passionate defiance. Not till the very close does the composition reach an expression of reconciliation and an inner brightening of mood.

It was undoubtedly this excessively agitated and painfully disturbed emotional content which promoted an exceptional concentration of Dvořák's creative powers, making the F minor Trio not only the most deeply unhappy and dark manifestation of the composer's spirit in his whole chamber music, but also one of the most significant of all his works in the range of its subject-matter and the complexity of its form. The music is generated from thoughts of unusual force, breadth and profundity, each movement providing a framework, the structure of which is as ingenious and original in detail as it is firm and bold in its general outline. The whole Trio is distinguished by an almost symphonic elevation of expression which, however, detracts nothing from its purely chamber music intimacy, and it was undoubtedly also this circumstance which led Dvořák to combine the two string instruments with the impressive volume of tone commanded by the piano.

The first movement (*Allegro ma non troppo*, F minor, $^4/_4$) opens in an atmosphere of bustling activity and preparation for battle with a strong admixture of pathos in the powerfully built-up climaxes of imposing majesty of thought and design. The thematic material is the most fertile and richly articulated of all. The principal theme consists of two independent periods, the first of which, gloomy but firmly contoured, is delivered by the violin and violoncello, closing with a kind of interrogation taken over by the piano and repeated with rising emphasis:

Without even waiting for an answer, the composer introduces the second period, an angry and again passionately repeated gesture of defiance:

Thereupon the piano returns to the first period, which has meantime regained its tranquility, passing by way of a short rhythmically related motif to the transitional thought 2.

The subordinate theme, reached through a new gradation based on motif 1*b*, falls again into two separate strains. The first, sung by the 'cello and then by the violin, has a long, expressive and steepiy oscillating emotional line; the other follows with an idea whose hard syncopations underline the expression of defiance:

The mood of stubborn resolve suggested by this motif is taken over and further intensified by the closing theme with its sharply pointed rhythms and air of majestic pride:

If the development working with the two strains of the principal theme (1*a* and 1*b*) is relatively short, its brevity is fully compensated by a further development of the same motifs, and also of the closing theme in a broadly designed and dynamic coda. This is grafted on to the recapitulation which diverges from the exposition in reversing the order of themes 2 and 1*b*.

The second movement *(Allegro grazioso,* C sharp minor, ²/₄) takes the place in this work of a Scherzo animated by Dvořák's usual warm impulsiveness and pawky humour, but a movement growing out of the general mood of the composition and following without any break in content on the one preceding. The spirit is weary after its exhausting struggle, but does not give in: over the monotonous accompaniment of staccato triplets, the protagonist hums a tune in which the persistently repeated and alternating rhythm of two semiquavers and one crotchet are still tinged with defiance, whimsical now rather than angry. This is the mood of the two perfectly symmetrical outer parts in which theme 5 is presented alternately by the piano and strings in a gay variety of keys:

The middle part of the movement offers a marked contrast to the outer parts in both mood and expression. Defiance has vanished and its place is taken by a dreamy pensiveness: above the gently sinuous accompaniment there flows a stream of calm, broad cantilena, in places with a strong undercurrent of emotion:

The slow third movement *(Poco adagio,* A flat major, $^4/_4)$ possesses rare beauty of melodic thought and the inspiration of deep emotional experience. There is a marked tranquilization as compared with the preceding movements, but the tone of spiritual suffering still permeates it. This is immediately perceptible in the line of the principal theme with which the violoncello opens the movement above the grave chords of the piano:

If in this theme we feel all the inner unhappiness of a sensitive spirit not yet inured to torturing doubts, the second, presented in canonic imitation in a dialogue between violin and violoncello, speaks in a tone of uncomplaining resignation, at first somewhat timidly and then, as the thought unfolds, modulating through G flat major into F major, with increasing fervour.

There is a return to theme 7 which, with its yearningly ardent song, concludes the first section of the three-part movement over the agitated groundwork of the piano which communicates its restlessness to the middle part, the first outburst—in G sharp minor—coming with the entry of a theme in hard, uncompromising rhythms and again in canonic imitation:

thereupon it continues in a calm, broad and wonderfully fervent song of consolation embodied in an exquisitely beautiful thought delivered by the violin first in B major and then again, shortly afterwards, in A flat major:

The third part opens in the same key but omits theme 7. This is, however, broadly treated in the short coda which, after a yearning reminiscence of theme 10, closes the movement with a delicate quotation of theme 8.

The fourth movement (*Allegro con brio*, F minor, $^3/_4$) returns, as far as content is concerned, to the stirring, fighting mood of the first movement, but is less prolific in themes, being based on a single pair. In general it keeps to the outlines of sonata form, but could also be interpreted as a rondo scheme (*a b a c a b a*) in which *c* stands for the development of the theme from part *a*. The expression of the principal theme is one of angry obstinacy. The opening descent of an octave has the air of a defiant stamp, and not less stubborn is the *furiant*-like alternation of duple and triple time. At

the close, however, as in the principal theme from the first movement (1), a characteristic rising interval forms an urgent mark of interrogation:

On this theme is built up the first broad paragraph of the movement, strongly agitated in mood and sharply accented in expression. Curiously stubborn, too, is the effect of the persistent repetition of the first three bars of the theme into which the strings interpolate the interrogative element:

A tranquilization sets in with a modulation through diminished seventh chords and, after a short transition, there enters in the key of C sharp minor the calmly vocal subordinate theme singing of uneasy feelings and a longing for all doubts to be resolved:

The mood does not last long, however, for with the return of the first theme (11), there is a return, too, of the original stir of battle. This mounts in the following part, worked out as a development of the elements in the first two bars of the same theme and of its final interrogation which, in a richly modulated gradation, makes itself heard more and more insistently. The climax opens into a recapitulation of the subordinate theme (12) delivering its unhappily questioning song in the tonic of F minor, whereupon the first theme (11) once more storms in. But this signals the end of the battle, for the waves of agitation now begin to subside and a broad coda, in spite of a number of dynamic culminations, finally presents the principal theme in a melodically greatly clarified form and in its transition to a major key:

At the very end of the movement, this expression is further softened by the entry of a strikingly harmonious major variant of the subordinate theme, which the 'cello follows up with a folk coloured reminiscence of the first theme:

An energetic unison cadence based on the principal theme (11) then confirms the impression that the work, which sang of a spiritual combat fought out on the battlefield of the composer's soul, must end with the expression of peace-bringing clarification and reconciliation.

THE "DUMKY" TRIO
for violin, violoncello and piano. — Opus 90.

Score begun in November 1890; the first Dumka completed on the 30th of the same month, the third completed on January 21st, the fourth on January 31st and the sixth on February 12th, 1891.—First performed by Ferdinand Lachner, Hanuš Wihan and the composer at an evening held by the Měšťanská beseda in Prague on April 11th, 1891, in celebration of the honorary degree conferred upon the composer by the Charles University.—Published by Simrock, 1894.—Duration: 35 minutes.

The "Dumky" Trio holds a special place not only in the series of Dvořák's trios but in his chamber music in general, a place comparable to that held by the "Slavonic Dances" in the body of the Master's orchestral composition. It is not in the usual cyclic sonata form, but is made up of a group of six movements each of which represents an art stylisation of a typical manifestation of Slav folk music, its originality and individuality being rendered with full plasticity through the highly distinctive expressive means of Dvořák's melodic, rhythmic and harmonic invention. Dvořák's well-known predilection for the Dumka form, in which a paragraph of pensively elegiac character alternates with a paragraph of riotous high spirits and whirling gaiety as in the Czardas, culminated here in the grouping of a whole series of these compositions, all of which are distinguished by remarkably expressiveness and beauty of thought, power of feeling and inner verve as well as by the characteristic tone-colouring in which, in keeping with the mood of the different Dumky, very happy use is made of the lovely dark lyrical tone of the violoncello.

Besides the different mood in which it is set, the Trio varies in one other feature from the "Slavonic Dances" with which it may be compared. Though they are written in simple two-part or three-part form, growing out of a single or at most two basic motifs, as a whole these Dumky are not a mere chance collection of six independent movements structurally unrelated and without a planned arrangement of content, as it might seem at first glance. A closer scrutiny shows that the first three Dumky are designed as a connected whole. Confirmation of this is found not only in the "attacca subito" after the first two, as compared with "a short pause" after the others, but in the logical unity of the content, from the cries of anguished lamentation to quiet mourning, followed by the heart-balm of consolation and reconciliation, and also in the strikingly close key relations: the first Dumka in E minor (at times E major) concluding in the key of C sharp minor in which the second Dumka remains throughout, while the third is set in A major. Whereas, too, the first three Dumky are distinguished by two strongly contrasted moods of lamentation and high-spirited gaiety, in the following only one of these elements predominates —in the fourth, calm melancholy, in the fifth, lively quick rhythms, while the last is again near in content and spirit to the first group. Thus, though the Trio is not an organically unified composition in sonata form in the strict sense of the word, there is still a clear tendency to keep to its main features in structure and mood. The first three inter-related Dumky may be looked upon as taking the place of the introductory movement in which sonata form is replaced by binary or ternary rondo form, the fourth Dumka has the character of a slow movement, just as the fifth has that of a Scherzo, while the last closes the work in the manner of a rondo finale.

The first Dumka is in two parts, based on a single theme whose melodic line is characterized by the large interval of ascending and descending sixths and rhythmically by the figure in the second last bar. In the first half *(Lento maestoso*, E minor, $^4/_8$), after a violoncello recitative of pronounced pathos accompanied by agitated passages in the piano, this basic theme appears first with an expression of anguished yearning in the violin, joined four bars later, by the violoncello in canonic imitation.

1a. Lento maestoso

In the next half of the Dumka, which doubles the pace *(Allegro quasi doppio movimento*, E major), the theme brightens into a major tonality and the mood turns gay with a counterpoint of bellike figurations in the piano.

Allegro

1b.

The diatonic descent of this figuration predominates in the further course of the movement of which it is the leading melody, dancing its way with fiery syncopations to the end of the paragraph. Both paragraphs—the grave and the gay, are repeated almost note for note but with a change of rôles in the instruments.

The second Dumka, also in two parts works with a pair of themes, the first of which falls again into two parts. The violoncello opens the movement with a delicate arpeggio in the piano and muted violin:

Poco adagio

2a.

The piano replies in a soothingly soft and melting cantilena in C sharp major:

The 'cello, however, continues its sad complaint, an expressive modulating process rather underlining the tone of lament, before it finally allows itself to be comforted. And as in the first Dumka, here, too, a second greatly accelerated section bursts in with a gay, folk-coloured theme in the violin:

over which the piano skips with a frolicking quaver figuration. This time the two parts of the Dumka are again repeated in a new instrumentation, the piano now having the chief say.

The third Dumka, in three-part form, manages with only one basic theme which, however, undergoes a variety of transformations in the course of the movement. This mood is, on the whole, brighter: the outer parts *(Andante,* A major, $^3/_4$) breathe the magic poetry of a summer evening bathed in moonlight and fragrant with the scent of ripening crops, leading the spirit away from sorrowful meditation of things past and dispelling relatively quickly the agitation underlying the quickening pace of the middle section *(Vivace non troppo,* A minor, $^2/_4$). After several calmly mystic introductory chords in the solo piano, there sounds, as it were from a distance, the pleasing song of the shepherd's pipe:

The theme is repeated in different variations, now more meditative, now more wistful, and yet again passionately ardent. A new variant in the violoncello, with the violin weaving a delicate figuration above it and supported by a bagpipe pedal point in the piano, opens the middle part in accelerated tempo:

A short swell of emotion disturbs the inner peace when the close of the theme develops into a resolute chromatically descending passage:

The return to the tonic key of A major, interwoven with a delight-ful episode sung rapturously by the violin, restores peace to the movement. A variant 3 *b*, beautifully coloured in its harmonies, then brings the Dumka to a close with an expression of tender meditation.

The fourth Dumka is simpler in mood, the prevailing tone being one of melancholy even though a livelier contrasting element is not lacking. The impression is strengthened by the fact that the calm, broadly exposed part returns several times as the main section, in a rondo scheme. The theme of this part *(Andante moderato*, D minor, $^2/_4$) which is somewhat reminiscent of Russian folk-song, is intro-duced first by the violoncello above an ostinato of a measured rhythm in the piano and monotonous quavers in the violin:

The 'cello continues its meditative song through four strophes, being interrupted twice by a kind of tripping, playful little tune in the piano *(Allegretto scherzando*, F major and D major):

and a third time by an explosively gay dance motif *(Allegro*, D major):

The prevailing melancholy of the mood is restored by the refined expression of the dreamily poetic conclusion.

The fifth Dumka is, except for a short meditative retardation, uniformly rapid in pace *(Allegro*, E flat major, $^6/_8$) and contrasts with the preceding Dumka in its strongly agitated rhythm, though the darkly passionate intensity of the theme and the occasional minor colouring of its variants remain in keeping with the basic mood of the whole cycle. The theme itself sets out impulsively in a syncopated rhythm, but is suddenly checked as if surprised by the sudden close into G major:

A more flexible variant then sways below light-running figurations in the piano (5*b*), and gives way, in its turn, to another variant with

characteristic canonic imitation, which again disturbs the expression
and passes from passionately forceful hard staccatos (5c) to a more
ardent lyrical line of melody (5d):

A lovely episode of recitative character based on the original version
of the theme (5a) only holds up for a short while the rapid pace of
the movement, which is resumed with the recapitulation of the preceding part with a complete recasting of the instrumental roles and
limiting itself to the exposition of the first three variants of the theme
(5a—c). The last of these (5c) then flowers into a delightful coda,
softly alluring in mood and winding up the Dumka with a resolute
flourish.

The sixth Dumka returns to the contrasted moods of the first
three Dumky built up on two alternating themes. The slow part
(*Lento maestoso*, C minor, $^4/_8$) with which the Dumka opens, works
with a thought of sorrowful character:

The close of this theme (bars 3 and 4) proves to be the germ of a new motif which provides the transition to a fiery *Vivace* and is the core of the thematic material in the quick part of the Dumka *(Vivace, $^2/_4$)*:

With the rhythm of this theme the Dumka resumes the slow tempo of the introductory Lento, first drawing out its main thought (6*a*) in a line of elegiac meditation:

and then presenting it in its original shape to open the recapitulation of the *Vivace*. An intimation that the work as a whole is drawing to its conclusion is the agitated augmentation of the principal theme *(Poco meno)* forming the transition to a thought in the major mode and to the final, whirling gradation which brings the composition to a brilliantly effective close.

V

COMPOSITIONS FOR TWO INSTRUMENTS

SONATA IN F MAJOR
for violin and piano.—Opus 57.

The first movement written in score between the 5th and the 6th, the second between the 9th and the 12th, and the third completed by the 17th March, 1880.—Published by Simrock, in 1880.—Duration: 23 minutes.

The Sonata for Violin and Piano, the only composition by Dvořák with that title, is a very intimate counterpart to the Violin Concerto in A minor which was written about the same time and has a similar content. It consists of three movements and is the purest of musical lyrics, prevailingly bright in mood and gaily animated in its conclusion.

The first movement *(Allegro ma non troppo*, F major, $^3/_4$) is in sonata form with two main themes, the so-called closing theme being only a rhythmic variant of the first not introducing any new melodic idea. The principal theme (1) which opens the composition is calm and idyllically refined, with a faintly Brahmsian melodic colouring:

The close is again, however, unmistakably Dvořák, as is also the following folk-coloured transitional motif developed out of its triplet figure:

On its second entry, the principal theme opens into a variant (1*b*) of which the rhythmic stylisation is later made use of in the function of a closing theme (1*c*):

Folk-music intonations also colour the playful subordinate theme which rather unexpectedly appears in D major instead of in C major:

In place of the closing theme, a canonic imitation is now worked out with sharply accented octave intervals (1*c*) whose rhythm, as already mentioned, is derived from the principal theme.

Then the nuances of mood determined by the character of the different themes quoted above alternate with gay variability in the development, working with themes 1, 1*a* and 2, and, later, in the fairly normal recapitulation with its clear and delicate character.

The second movement *(Poco sostenuto,* A major, $^6/_4$), comparatively not very extended, and roughly in two-part form, proceeds throughout in broad $^6/_4$ time, its warmly emotional cantilena divided evenly between the violin and the piano. Whereas the first theme (3) shows in the main a falling tendency in pitch-apart from the small disturbing rhythmic figure either in quavers (3*a*) or triplets (3*b*)—the second theme, exposed in a dialogue between the two instruments, describes a rising curve in which a crotchet phrase is usually answered by a quaver phrase (4).

This part, based on these two themes, is followed without transition by a somewhat abridged and calm recapitulation, despite a strongly emotional gradation, and concludes delicately with an expression of dreamy tenderness.

The third movement *(Allegro molto,* F major, $^2/_4$) is again in sonata form, but is built up on three independent themes of which the first is unaffectedly happy, both in melody and rhythm, and characteristically Czech in expression:

The other two themes are quieter in movement and melodically more beguiling:

espress.

The basically lively character of the movement is, however, not affected by these themes, which appear in more humorous and rhythmically flexible transformations, the first of them, the subordinate theme (6), already in its own exposition, and then the other, the closing theme (7), in a lively development section. The whole movement ends in a mood of lively excitement and good humour.

SONATINA IN G MAJOR
for violin and piano.—Opus 100.

Written in sketch between November 19th and 22nd, the first movement in score between November 23rd and 24th, the second and third completed by November 25th and the fourth by December 3rd, 1893, all in New York.— Dedicated "To my Children."—Published by Simrock in 1894.—Duration: 18 minutes.

The Sonatina in G major is the last of Dvořák's chamber music works to be written on American soil. It does not bear the opus number 100 merely by chance, for the composer chose as this jubilee work a small composition of the greatest intimacy as regards content, and dedicated it to his own children, the ten-year-old Toník and the fifteen-year-old Otilka, with due consideration for their capabilities as performers. The character of the Sonatina is aptly described by Dvořák himself in a letter dated 2. I. 1894 to his publisher Simrock, in which he wrote: "It is intended for young people (dedicated to my children) but grown-ups, too, let them get what enjoyment they can out of it..." Both in its moderate technical demands and in its content, the Sonatina is clearly adapted to the powers and capacity of young people. Yet the task of composition is carried out with a full sense of its seriousness and with such apparent creative delight and spontaneity that it cannot but fill the hearts of older people, too, with delight.

All four small movements of the Sonatina are simple in form and very neatly designed, but not without interesting digressions from the traditional schemes in the structure and in the handling of the thematic material. The mood of the Sonatina is delightfully young and fresh, in places full of rollicking fun and good spirits, yet not without passages of pensive melancholy and wistfulness such as are a feature of all Dvořák's compositions written in America. To the place of its origin must also be attributed the "American" traits in the themes (pentatonic scale, minor seventh in the minor mode, syncopated rhythms etc.) which, however, are made use of in the composition in a way that is as typically Dvořák as is the naive charm of the whole sonata.

The first movement *(Allegro risoluto,* G major, ³/₄) swings out with vigorous step and is written in sonata form comprising three themes. The first is, itself, a three-part song based on three thematic elements and spread over thirty-two bars:

This principal theme leads straight into the subordinate theme. It is in the key of E minor and in the form of a dialogue between the two instruments in imitation above an undulating triplet accompaniment (note the characteristic minor seventh marked ×):

The triplet figure and the melancholy minor mode is taken over by the closing theme, its expression gaining in strength and energy:

The relatively short development works mainly with the beginning or the principal theme (1) in the "skočná" rhythm of the piano bass which contributes most of all to the cheerful fresh mood of the movement. The recapitulation is extended to include a perfectly tranquil coda with which the movement dreamily dies away.

The second movement *(Larghetto,* G minor, $^2/_4$) is a gentle lullaby designed on a symmetrical pattern as regards mood and partly also in form. The introductory melody, which Dvořák is said to have noted down while watching the impressive natural spectacle of the famous Minnehaha Falls beside the town of St. Paul, Minnesota (4. IX. 1893), is full of heart-sick yearning and a deep sadness:

The expression then brightens somewhat when the continuation of the beautifully vocal melody shifts into B flat major, in which key a song grows out of two new motifs (5*a* and 5*b*) tinged with a sweet, sad longing:

This is the mood, too, of the short intermezzo in G major, more lively in pace and drawn over a pedal point of a tonic fifth, it has an innocent simplicity of expression and a bell-like clarity of tone:

A return to the mood of the first part, limited now to a quotation of the melancholy introductory theme (4), concludes the movement without, however, dispelling its sadness.*

The third movement *(Molto vivace, G major, ³/₄)* is a gay and very charming little Scherzo, Mozartian both in form and treatment. The outer completely symmetrical parts are rhythmically more sparkling, in keeping with the character of the song-theme in two strains:

* Perhaps the lyrical, emotional character of the melody explains why this slow movement became so popular as to acquire an independent existence. In any case, its popularity induced Simrock to publish the movement separately in a great variety of instrumental arrangements and without the composer's authorisation, under all sorts of titles such as "Indian Canzonetta", "Indian Lament", "Indian Lullaby" etc.

7 b.

The Trio is quieter in movement and more appealing in the first eight bars (8a), but then becomes more agitated with the appearance of sharply accented syncopations (8b):

8 a. Trio

8 b.

The fourth movement *(Allegro*, G major, $^2/_4$) returns to sonata form and shows a predilection for light-heartedly discursive themes. The very fresh and youthful expression of the principal theme (9c) is underlined by a syncopated stamp in the third bar, which recurs (more insistently in the transitional thought 9b):

9 a. Allegro

9 b.

The subordinate theme, here as in the first movement is in the key of E minor and trips lightly in that "skočná" tapping rhythm which was noted as being typically "American" in the String Quintet in E flat major, op. 97 (See ex. 8a on p. 43):

10.

pp

All the more interesting then is the closing theme which unexpectedly builds up to an independent paragraph contrasting with the preceding one, both in its more melting and softly dreamy melodic line as well as in its transposition to the major mode and in its quieter pace *(Molto tranquillo,* E major). Its whole exposition is one of the loveliest passages in the Sonatina and, especially in its middle period (11*b*), is coloured with the expression of romantic longing which was undoubtedly prompted by the composer's longing for his far-off native land:

The development, while drawing exclusively upon the figures of the principal theme (9*a*), again revives the original youthful freshness of mood which is maintained unflaggingly throughout the recapitulation (with the subordinate theme in G minor), except for the new broad presentation of the closing theme (11*a*—*c*) which has a deeply vibrant undertone of emotion. Out of the first two bars of the principal theme, there grows a coda in which a dynamic build-up of tone, along with an acceleration of tempo, bring the sonata to a close in a mood of hearty and unaffected gaiety.